# PRAISE FOR JENNIFER THOMPSON

Jennifer Thompson brilliantly shepherds us on a workplace safari identifying the Martyrs, Victims and Jerks we encounter in our professional habitats. Through awareness, humor and honesty we gain the confidence to courageously look in the mirror and make changes for the better, both professionally and personally.

GIULIA CAPPELLI, AUTHOR, *FIND PEACE ON PURPOSE*

Jennifer has worked closely with many areas including the leadership team, sales and marketing, and frontline supervisors. We have seen the impact of Jennifer's strategy of transferring training back on the job. Jennifer takes an upfront and personal approach to her training and coaching. Her passion and caring shine through each and every project she has completed.

GLORIA FLORES, VICE PRESIDENT OF HUMAN RESOURCES

Jennifer Thompson has the qualities of an engineer, scientist, educator, entrepreneur, psychologist, and marriage counselor. This makes her uniquely qualified to delve into the minds of people who call themselves "managers." Through a variety of case studies, she brings to light their shadows and, more importantly, provides us mere mortals the means to deal with these personalities. On top of that, she's a dog lover, so she must know what she's talking about!

JAMES M. KAUFMAN, PH.D. IN PHYSICS<br>FROM CALTECH

# MARTYRS, VICTIMS AND JERKS

## DEALING WITH TROUBLE IN THE WORKPLACE

JENNIFER THOMPSON

TIME4THOMPSON

Copyright © 2025 Jennifer Thompson

The information provided in this book is for informational purposes only and is not intended as a substitute for professional mental health advice, diagnosis, or treatment. Always seek the advice of your physician or other qualified mental health provider with questions you may have regarding a medical condition or mental health issue. NEVER DISREGARD PROFESSIONAL MEDICAL ADVICE OR DELAY IN SEEKING IT BECAUSE OF SOMETHING YOU HAVE READ IN THIS BOOK. IF YOU ARE IN CRISIS OR THINK YOU MAY HAVE AN EMERGENCY, CALL YOUR DOCTOR OR EMERGENCY SERVICES IMMEDIATELY.

All rights reserved. No part of this book may be reproduced, distributed, or transmitted in any form or by any means, including photocopying, recording, or other electronic or mechanical methods, without the prior written permission of the publisher, except with brief quotations embodied in critical reviews and certain other noncommercial uses permitted by copyright law. For permission requests, contact the publisher at the email address below.

**Publisher: Time4Thompson nomvj.com info@nomvj.com**

ISBN: 979-8-9922420-0-3; Kindle ASIN: B0F3VB16RG; EPUB 979-8-9922420-1-0

Library of Congress Control Number: 2025906930

The names and identifying details of some individuals in this book have been changed to protect their privacy. While the author has made every effort to ensure the accuracy of the information herein, the author does not assume and hereby disclaims any liability to any party for any loss, damage, or disruption caused by errors or omissions, whether such errors or omissions result from negligence, accident, or any other cause.

Illustrations: Dr. Christopher Zeineh

Book cover and interior design: La Puerta Productions

Editor: Gerald Everett Jones

Copyeditor: Jason Letts

Research Assistant / Proofreader: Adero Joan Cate

*For Mom, Dad, Tom, and my dear Koda*

# CONTENTS

A message from the author — ix

**PART ONE**
**WELCOME TO THE JUNGLE**
How Did We Get Here? — 3

**PART TWO**
**MARTYRS**
I'm a Galápagos Islands Martyr — 9
The High-Performing Martyr — 17
Not Awkward — Exceptional! — 19
Observe the Office Martyr in Their Habitat — 21
More Consequences of Being a Martyr — 24
Understanding the Workaholic Martyr — 28
When Martyrs Complain — 31
Hard Time Saying "NO!" — 38
Playing the Social Scientist at the Office — 44
From Martyrs to Victims — 48

**PART THREE**
**VICTIMS**
The Office Victim — 53
Sad, Sad Susan — 55
It's a Family Tradition — 58
RIP for the RFP — 60
Rumors of Layoffs — 64
The Covid Experience — 67
Madison and Hanna — 69
Impostors — 71
Manage Your Mindset — 75

Victims' Dilemma — Dealing with a Jerk     83
When You Feel Like a Victim     88

PART FOUR
## JERKS

What About This Book Grabbed You?     97
Jerks Are Bullies     101
Kevin the Bully     103
Intimidation and Efficiency     110
The Unwritten Rule     115
Traveling with the CEO Jerk     118
Working for a Jerk Can Be Deadly     123
Jerk Bosses Cost More than Hurt Feelings     126
Dave the Mindful Jerk     129
The Tardy and Unprepared Jerk     133
The Entitled Jerk     136
The Jerk Customer     139
Kiss-Up, Kick-Down Jerks     143

PART FIVE
## WHERE DO WE GO FROM HERE?

Get Your Bearings     155
Conducting Your Own Self-Assessment     157
Asking Yourself the Key Questions     162
Conducting a Workplace Assessment     174
Taking Action — Your Field Guide     176
Toward a Healthier and Happier Workplace     184
References and Further Reading     189
Acknowledgments     193
About the Author     195

# A MESSAGE FROM THE AUTHOR

A portion of the book's earnings will go to the ***Elephant Matriarch Project.***

After meeting its founder, Georja Umano, I could not imagine a better cause to partner with, not because of the obvious link to the African safari theme, but because of the true heroes of a bigger story: In Africa today, there is an alarming decimation of elephants and other African wildlife. Here is a new opportunity of saving them by enlisting rural, impoverished young mothers who are trained in programs at the Elephant Matriarch Project to become their protectors and guardians.

Thank you for the purchase of this book, and please consider how you can further support the Elephant Matriarch Project (elephantmatriarch.org).

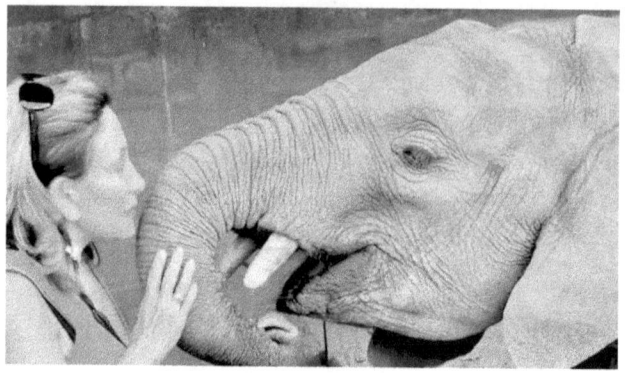

### *A message from Georja Umano, Founder, Elephant Matriarch Project*

In rural areas throughout Africa today, there are literally millions of "forgotten girls" who have gotten pregnant too early, dropped out of school and, for the most part, lost track of opportunities for further education or career advancement--way before they had a chance to explore their options. Our project aims to guide them and give them back those opportunities while at the same time to create with them a new stratum of African society who are impassioned about saving elephants and other endangered wildlife.

Jennifer, in her generosity has offered to donate a portion of her book sales from **Victims, Martyrs and Jerks** to Elephant Matriarch Project. We are just getting started, and I and my partners are very grateful for this help. It is of tremendous importance to us both for the financial aspect as well as the publicity. We, global citizens need to know and understand what is happening to our world: as we lose our precious wildlife, we are also losing the brain and empathetic contributions of millions of girls by limiting their possibilities.

Please join us in our quest for a successful pilot program and resources to spread and multiply.

Thank you to Jennifer and all her wonderful readers!

*Georja Umano*

**Elephant Matriarch Project Mission Statement**

The Elephant Matriarch Project is an educational and vocational project for young, undereducated mothers, their children, and their community. Its aim is to lift up an under-served population, and by offering inspiring and practical information as well as academic advancement — to improve their security, know-how, knowledge and love of animals and the environment while ensuring their vocational futures.

https://elephantmatriarch.org

PART ONE

## WELCOME TO THE JUNGLE

*Not until we are lost do we begin to find ourselves.*

- Henry David Thoreau

## BEFORE WE SET OUT...
## YOUR SAFARI GUIDE WANTS YOU TO KNOW

The information provided in this book is for informational purposes only and is not intended as a substitute for professional mental health advice, diagnosis, or treatment.

Always seek the advice of your physician or other qualified mental health provider with questions you may have regarding a medical condition or mental health issue.

Never disregard professional medical advice or delay in seeking it because of something you have read in this book. If you are in crisis or think you may have an emergency, call your doctor or emergency services immediately.

## YOU CAN LOOK FORWARD TO A FASCINATING EXPERIENCE!

## HOW DID WE GET HERE?

**Congratulations! You are heading out on a journey!**

Many years back, before my first (and sadly only) African safari, the guide handed me a book. It was titled, *The Big Five*, and the pages were filled with fascinating details about the habits and habitats of the five animals every visitor hopes to see while on safari. I invite you to do the same.

You now hold the guidebook for discovering and grasping our Big Three: Martyr, Victim, and Jerk. I'm honored to serve as your scout as we begin this adventure. I will help you navigate rough, untamed roads so you can see the "wild" in your life in its most natural state.

Like a parched journey (herd of giraffe) on the move for a watering hole in the middle of a drought, we must also leave our comfort zones to gain awareness and bring hope where it is scarce. So, get ready; we are traveling deep into open office spaces, closed meetings, and corner offices on a fact-finding safari.

Bushwhacking a new path demands courage.

I will challenge you to reinforce boundaries, affirming that your time and environment are sacred and worthy of protection.

Just as there are signs on a game reserve fence warning poachers to keep out, you too must become unapologetically comfortable with your own fences. These fences aid to keep the poachers of your well-being — the martyrs, victims, and jerks — at a safe and manageable distance.

Let's take a closer look at our Big Three. For now, they are still safely caged; I won't release you to the wild of your workplace until you know exactly how to spot and manage them!

If you have been wondering what mammals make up the Big Five, they are the African lion, the Cape buffalo, the African leopard, the black rhinoceros, and the African elephant.

**Spoiler Alert**

The Big Five of Africa may seem tame compared to what awaits you in the world of Martyrs, Victims, and Jerks!

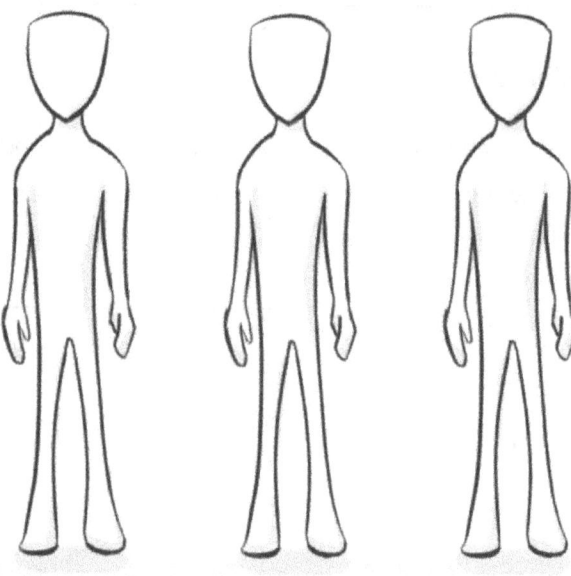

Welcome to the World of the Martyr! They walk among you.

# PART TWO

# MARTYRS

*I have lived on the lip of insanity,
wanting to know reasons, knocking on a door.
It opens.
I've been knocking from the inside.*

- **Rumi**

# IDENTIFY THE MARTYR

| | |
|---|---|
| **Behaviors** | Martyrs believe no one works as hard as they do. They will sacrifice themselves for a cause but then quickly resent it. The "Blame Game" allows them to avoid taking responsibility for anything wrong. **They are experts at making others feel guilty.** |
| **Key Indicators** | You may have a martyr on your hands if they:<br><br>• Refuse to accept responsibility for the decisions that have caused them to suffer<br>• Actively campaign that they are righteous and self-sacrificing<br>• Have a tough time saying *no* and setting personal boundaries<br>• Do not solve their problems<br>• Constantly seeking appreciation, recognition, and attention for work done |
| **Background** | When we hear the word *martyr*, we might think of the noble acts of Mahatma Gandhi and Mother Teresa—Gandhi for his relentless nonviolent stance against colonialism and Mother Teresa for her saintly care of the sick and underprivileged in Calcutta. Looking further back in history, some hailed Joan of Arc for her bravery, while her adversaries burned her at the stake.<br><br>Take notice of the self-inflicted immolation of the office martyr and their campaign of endless suffering. |
| **Identified** ☐ | Check this box when you feel confident that you have identified a Martyr, including yourself. |

# I'M A GALÁPAGOS ISLANDS MARTYR

**I will tell you when I first realized I was a martyr knocking from the inside.**

It's a true story, one that came at significant cost to my ego and ultimately inspired this book.

Was the book *On the Origin of Species* required reading for you in school? For me, it was in ninth grade, and a book I had dreaded opening soon became my refuge. Charles Darwin took me into a world of wonder filled with mysteries and adventure. Imagine a tortoise the size of a table and birds with blue feet! As a fourteen-year-old, I declared that one day I would see it all for myself, not just pictures in a book but with my own feet planted beside the blue-footed booby on the sands of the Galápagos Islands.

Years later, when I pried myself away from a busy office, my Darwin dream could finally come true.

After a long journey from California to Guayaquil, Ecuador, I boarded a small boat with a tour group to cross from the mainland to the islands. On the beach ahead, seagulls wheeled overhead, and mischievous seals played carelessly in the surf, mirroring the joy I hoped to feel as I began my long-awaited evolutionary exploration. Standing at the ship's bow, the salty spray hit my face as I leaned into the wind. The vessel was small and cozy, the kind where passengers quickly learned each other's names. Our guide, a biologist named Miguel, was no exception-warm, approachable, and ready to prepare us for the daily excursions that awaited.

> **Heads Up!**
>
> **KEEP HANDS AND FEET INSIDE THE VEHICLE**

After dropping my bags in my room, I quickly rushed to hear Miguel give the group our first briefing with an introduction to the ship. Miguel was a renowned biologist whose face I recognized from National Geographic. After all those years, I'd get to now ask my questions that had vexed me since ninth grade in person to Miguel! Miguel gave the go-ahead to open the floor to questions. In response, hungry for knowledge, we passengers quickly raised our hands. Starting the inquisition, a woman loudly asked, "How many species of birds inhabit the islands?" Then another inquired, "How old is Lonesome George, and was he a pet of Charles Darwin's?"

I raised my hand. Miguel smiled and called on me. "This boat has Wi-Fi, yes?" I said, standing up, my tone more demanding than curious.

> **BOOK4U**
>
> Charles Darwin
>
> On Origin of Species

The disappointment on Miguel's face was clear as he considered my question.
"No, there is no Wi-Fi, but the boat does have a satellite phone that works, sometimes, not often, but sometimes. The reception is poor at best."

Those words shifted my focus from learning about the secrets of humankind's evolution to figuring out how I could be available when the chance arose to place a call using the ship's shoddy satellite system.

---

Instead of asking how the blue-footed booby came to have blue feet, I was more concerned with the proper longitudinal and latitudinal alignment of a drifting boat in the middle of the Pacific Ocean.

> **Heads Up!**
>
> **YOUR GUIDE SHOULD HAVE A PHONE -**
>
> **YOURS!**

Do you know that annoying person who repeatedly asks on long road trips, "Are we there yet?" I was that person. I don't know if it was that I didn't notice or I didn't care that I was capsizing our gentle skipper's patience with my constant pestering.

It was hard to fully enjoy this dream trip while my thoughts kept drifting back to work. Too concerned about making contact, I didn't do the math in my head about how much these calls cost me. While Miguel informed me that passengers could phone the mainland for twenty dollars per minute, I didn't hear the actual numbers, I just heard it was possible. Over the course of the trip, I made six separate calls, each averaging about nine minutes. Do the math, and those aquatic connections added up to $1,080. I felt it was a small price to pay to reassure my clients that, while I may be drifting around the Galápagos Islands, they were always on my mind!

Upon returning fresh from the trip of a lifetime, I could not wait to see my clients. I felt as proud as a child with a perfect report card, eager to hear praise for selfless work completed. What would they say when I came back? I expected comments such as, "Jen, it's commendable that you'd call us from the Galápagos!"

> **Heads Up!**
>
> **YOUR GUIDE WILL OFFER LOTS OF TIPS**
>
> **AND EXPECTS ONLY ONE FROM YOU**

Instead, upon my return to the office, the first words from a key client were, "Jen, get a life and never do that again!"

This wasn't the payoff I was looking for. Their statement hurt. I wanted recognition. When I called my clients from the Galápagos, my intention was to prove my commitment and willingness to sacrifice my dream vacation for them. Surely, if they saw how hard I was working, at such personal cost, they would acknowledge my dedication and reward my sainthood.

But I came to realize that's not what they wanted. They never asked for what I willingly offered.

> **Heads Up!**
>
> **DON'T DISTURB THE ANIMALS**

When I left for vacation, my manager and staff wished me well. No one expected me to take time away from my trip to check in. No, my compulsion to check in originated from my need to prove myself. Had you tried to stop me from dialing that satellite phone in the Pacific Ocean, I would have snapped at you faster than a famished tortoise going after a fresh leafy green.

Although I didn't get the reward I expected, this experience forced me to examine my intentions and consider how many times I had missed *a moment* because I was thinking about that satellite phone.

In our daily lives, it's not about the satellite phone.

It's about the everyday ways we slip into the role of the martyr.

---

**What have you missed out on while fretting about your own "connection to the mainland"?**

---

One fundamental truth stands out: martyrs expect a payoff for their suffering. I felt disappointed when my clients didn't shower the expected glory on me. Take note: if martyrs do not receive the payoff they expect, bitterness often follows. I can speak from experience.

The good news (if we are aware) is that the discomfort allows us to examine our intentions. No one asked me to make such a sacrifice on my vacation. No, my orders didn't come from management or clients but from a small voice urging me to prove myself, yet again. Instead of questioning the intention, I focused on the orders.

> **Reality Check**
> I'm not alone. An estimated 5.26 million employees put in overtime every year that they are not compensated for – a clear sign of martyrdom.

The way out of this dilemma begins with recognizing when we slip into martyr-like behaviors. Of course, it is easier to identify these behaviors in our family, our coworkers, or our even our neighbors.

Because self-examination is more difficult, rest assured that I included a self-assessment in the last part of this book for the martyr complex and two other troublesome types.

## THE ORIGIN STORY OF THE OFFICE MARTYR

**Martyrs take pride in their status, and over time it can become their identity.**

To martyrs who crave recognition, the workplace often becomes the easiest place to find it — perhaps because they do not feel truly appreciated in other areas of their lives.

Psychologists often link the martyr complex to childhood self-esteem. Martyrs frequently feel inadequate and can probably remember when they did as a child also.

Let's be clear, no one benefits from low self-esteem. When you find it in yourself, you may wish others could see and have empathy for what caused the hit to our esteem. Therefore, when you observe it in others, realize that rebuking or critiquing them probably will not improve their likability or output. That approach wouldn't work on us, why would it work on someone else?

> **Reality Check**
> Psychotherapist Rachel Shattock Dawson has said that martyrdom can be addictive, and the consequences are disappointment, resentment, and anger.

**Fun Facts**

The distinctive blue feet of blue-footed boobies come from carotenoid pigments in fresh fish, which change the collagen structure in their skin.

Lonesome George (1910-2012) was not a pet or alive when Charles Darwin visited the Galápagos. He was the last of his species, and I missed seeing him by just a few months, although I don't know if I would have been present enough to appreciate him fully. Ironically, he lived on Darwin Island- where, unlike my boat, there was plenty of telephone service.

# THE HIGH-PERFORMING MARTYR

**Here's another personal story of when I leaned fully into my martyrdom.**

As a director of a global team, I was unaware of how my choices affected my coworkers. Some call it *flow down*. Consider whether you want to be at the bottom of Mount Kilimanjaro if it erupts with scalding hot lava.

Sixteen-hour workdays, fueled by coffee and under-desk naps in dark offices, were my routine long before tech CEOs made it cool. I had a reputation as a top performer that I was not going to lose. I was also the ICU patient, with an IV in one arm and a cell phone in the hand of the other. Hindsight provides 20/20 vision of how unhealthy this was for me.

I wanted desperately to prove how invaluable I was, yet at the same time fearing being inadequate. A perpetual cycle of fear-fed work and recognition. It wasn't as if I were curing cancer, but I convinced myself my work was just as critical, driving me into an unsustainable downward spiral.

My identity had become rooted in being a high-performing martyr. I thought having high-performance martyr as a brand was impressive. Until a bad dream made me turn the binoculars on myself.

One night in the ER, a nightmare jolted me awake. In the haziness of that loud, chaotic room, I dreamed I was overhearing an employee at dinner with her family.

I can't say exactly what I heard in my dream (this is a PG-rated book), but I'll share the essence. It is called the *ripple effect*.

The ripple effect is when your actions affect others, deliberately or not. Being a high-performing martyr not only took an effect on me, but it was also hurting those around me. When is the last time you considered how your actions (or inactions) affect others?

> **Reality Check**
> If someone in your office called you a martyr, would you take it as a compliment? Survey says no: Seventy-three percent of those polled in a recent workplace survey said martyr would be a putdown, not a compliment.

# NOT AWKWARD — EXCEPTIONAL!

**Spoiler Alert**

Low self-esteem can make a person particularly vulnerable to bullying.

As an awkward, husky kid growing up in a town of athletes and beauty queens (or so I thought at the time), I was like a Thompson gazelle, constantly evading hyenas. Much like the camouflage an African deer relies on for survival, I developed my own coping mechanism to not be seen, retreating into the restroom to eat my lunch. Those red stalls and white sinks became my safe cove, as I needed to hide from predators that would definitely harass me for the outrageous act of eating a sandwich.

**Fun Fact**

Most mammals won't consume food where they relieve themselves.

---

> **Heads Up!**
>
> **A GAME DRIVE IS NOT A GAME**

As the lunch bell rang, I donned my armor and braced for battle (cue the John Barry score from Out of Africa). My next stop was English class, where I poured everything I had into my work. I painstakingly typed my homework on my Commodore 64's primitive word processor. The feeling of tearing the homework along the perforated edge still sticks in my mind. The paper cuts I collected over time became tiny battle scars- a testament to my bravery.

My belief was that performing well in class would keep me safe and maybe even deter the apex predators roaming the hallways of the school from an attack.

That same need to prove myself eventually shifted — from producing impressive homework in school to taking on more than I could handle in the workplace.

> **BOOK4U**
>
> Mayo Clinic Staff,
>
> *"Self-Esteem Check: Too Low, Too High, or Just Right?"*
>
> Mayo Clinic

# OBSERVE THE OFFICE MARTYR IN THEIR HABITAT

Perhaps you haven't noticed the martyr motives in yourself, yet. So, grab your binoculars and observe your colleagues and supervisors for signs of martyrdom. Let's listen to a conversation at work that could be a martyr in the making.

Does this workplace chat sound familiar?

"Hey, Steve, how are you doing?"

Steve snaps back, "How am I doing? I was here for eighteen hours yesterday. They still haven't fixed the copier to make two-sided copies. No one is ready for the conference next week; I will have to work on it all weekend. However, that's fine. It's what I do."

> **Reality Check**
> Citing Dr. Dawson on psychology once again, martyrs think their sacrifice will get them noticed. But what they are more likely to bring on themselves is resentment from their coworkers. It's a vicious cycle, which can spill over into the person's private life and perhaps lead to depression.

It sounds like Steve is having a terrible week. In fact, every week must be terrible because Steve usually responds in this way, wanting to make sure everyone notices his sacrifice.

While Steve's hard work seems beneficial, his overboard behavior comes with disadvantages that you may not see on the surface.

Managers might seem to like this person's early arrival and late departure, particularly if they're salaried and not paid overtime. But there are serious downsides to the seemingly selfless employee. Consistently agreeing to every request can lead to an overwhelming workload, which eventually reduces the quality of work. When quality is questioned, so is trust, and fingers start pointing. Spoiler alert — the martyr will start blaming others.

According to sociologist Nancy Aldrich, the behavior of an Office Martyr can harm colleagues, teams, and the entire organization. Office Martyrs may subtly imply that their increased workload is because their coworkers are such predictable slackers. Team members might then feel guilty, leading to overwork or resignation. The results often include decreased productivity, lower efficiency, and weakened morale — sometimes driving away employees and maybe customers as well.

> **Reality Check**
> Dr. Wilson Wong, senior researcher at The Work Foundation, warns that workers who don't seek promotions may feel they have no bargaining power. As a result, they may feel their only alternative is to complain constantly. They thus seek benefit from the praise of their coworkers, if not from their managers.

The martyr's complaints are detrimental to everyone within listening distance.

Here's some expert advice if you or someone you know is considering taking on too much:

---

**The Organization for Economic Co-operation and Development (OECD)** found that employees with the highest productivity tend to work the fewest hours — probably because their work is efficient and highly motivated!

---

We can agree that being busy is not the same as being productive. We can also agree that you won't likely have a manager who agrees that you should work less hours to be more productive. Just take notice. Where are you spending time that is not paying off? Maybe it is getting stuck in a martyrs' trap!

---

**I'm your guide, and I'll help you avoid martyr traps and danger.** Remember the rule of getting out of quicksand? Don't fight it- if you get pulled in, the key is to move slowly and deliberately until you're free. The same is true when an Office Martyr tries to snare you with their stories of sainthood. Resist the struggle, and instead, ease your way out with calm, intentional steps.

---

# MORE CONSEQUENCES OF BEING A MARTYR
## (OR ENDURING ONE)

**Here's a case study that underscores the pitfalls of martyrdom.**

Barbara was a successful executive at a well-known pharmaceutical company. After a productive year, the office was, as usual, closed for the Christmas holiday. She was the last to leave the office most nights, and Christmas Eve was no exception. Her development team was working on an important project due in February of the new year. Because they were ahead of schedule, the team was rewarded with a half-day off to finish their holiday preparations.

Barbara, however, frowned at her team's early departures, though she kept quiet. She reflected on her career. She had risen to the executive ranks by rarely leaving early or taking time off. Why should Christmas Eve be different?

# MORE CONSEQUENCES OF BEING A MARTYR

Around 10:00 p.m., Barbara took a brief break to give her team a status update and sent the team this text:

> Team, I'm sure you're spending a pleasant Christmas Eve with family tonight. I should be out of the office by the time the clock strikes midnight. Just so you know, the project timeline is updated, and it's on SharePoint now. Best, Barbara

What do you think Barbara's intentions were? Was she really hoping her team would print out the revised project schedule and display it proudly at Christmas dinner? Probably not. She could have just updated and uploaded without the flashing neon sign that screamed:

> Hey, it's Christmas Eve, and I'm working. What are you doing?

It is a little like imagining Mother Teresa in Calcutta's slums emailing at 3:00 a.m. Rome time.

> Your Holiness Pius XII, Cardinals, Bishops, and Vatican City staff, I know it's late, and you are probably sleeping, but I just wanted to let you know that all the children have been fed, and tomorrow, I will focus my efforts on the lepers.

Thinking back on Barbara's email, what kind of ripple effect do you think it had?

Feelings of guilt or resentment would be understandable.

If either of these were innate responses to her message, the overall health of the team would suffer.

1. They expect us to work during the holidays.
2. I can't do this anymore. I will check out Indeed.com to see who is hiring.

But in the hypothetical case of Mother Teresa, the pope might have told the cardinals:

> That poor woman works too hard. It's time to bring her home!

Another official could have proposed:

> Yes, but who will we find to do that much work?

---

I'm not against working extra hours when they're truly necessary and unavoidable — we all understand the pressure of deadlines. But I encourage you to seek help if possible. Your team will likely be willing to assist, and they may even feel valued when you trust them enough to ask.

So, what are you working on that you could use some help with? Challenge the part of yourself that resists reaching out to ask for help.

### Is Anti-Martyr Your Brand?

Alternatively, not sharing your hard work, though potentially virtuous, could lead to a lack of recognition. I've seen many hardworking employees miss out on promotions to less capable, but more outspoken coworkers because they don't advocate for themselves.

---

**It is time to interrupt this natural evolutionary path.**

---

**Heads Up!**

**THESE CRITTERS DON'T WORK FOR PEANUTS**

# UNDERSTANDING THE WORKAHOLIC MARTYR

**Our communication and coping skills develop in our younger years.** Digging deeper into the existing research connecting martyrdom and childhood, I had a sudden realization: certain employees HR had assigned to me clearly fit the pattern.

**Reality Check**

People who say little and listen more in meetings are often perceived as being smarter than the talkers.

At the core of martyrdom is a lack of self-esteem. Despite boasting about their sacrifices, martyrs may secretly be questioning their own worth. A typical childhood fear that we bring into adulthood involves anxieties about feeling inadequate. Yet, even as we make progress, we focus on our shortcomings and mistakes. When in martyr mode, we struggle to recognize our own skills, knowledge, and accomplishments. These deeply rooted, long-established beliefs can be shifted. It takes commitment to tear out those old roots and plant new beliefs that we are good enough.

When I was working eighty-hour weeks, I don't recall celebrating many wins, despite numerous successes. I just earned myself a hospital visit. Eventually, if we are aware, we understand that our well-being is our own responsibility. I was just a slow learner.

While I considered my high-achieving peers and role models, it was eye-opening when one shared with me (years later) that she looked successful on the outside but was drowning on the inside. Remember that flow down and ripple effect I mentioned earlier? This executive was eventually let go after too many employee complaints came across the HR desk. Her team members were gradually recruited from outside the organization.

> **Reality Check**
>
> Project managers use **SWOT** in their Gate Reviews to analyze their team's:
>
> **S**trengths
>
> **W**eaknesses
>
> **O**bstacles
>
> **T**hreats

> **Reality Check**
>
> A Pitch Deck is a slide show used to sell an idea or product by showing rather than telling - and as concisely as possible.

Poaching occurs on game reserves and in every corner of the natural world, robbing the planet and your company of rare specimens.

Burned-out and disgruntled employees are easy prey for recruiters.

**But what happens if they stay — and continue to complain?**

# WHEN MARTYRS COMPLAIN

**Here's an example of the consequences of a complaining martyr.**

A Cherokee grandfather imparted wisdom to his grandson through a tale of two wolves.

He began, "There is a fight going on inside of me. The terrible fight is happening between two wolves. One is evil. This wolf is angry, envious, arrogant, and acts superior.

The other wolf is good. He is joyful, peaceful, hopeful, humble, kind, and empathetic.

That very battle rages within you and everyone else.

"Which wolf will win?" the grandson asked.

The Cherokee elder replied, "The wolf you feed."

> **BOOK4U**
>
> Travis Bradberry,
>
> "How Complaining Rewires Your Brain for Negativity,"
>
> TalentSmart

This allegory is an example of the function of our subconscious. Our thoughts shape our choices, and our choices shape our behavior.

What role does our thinking play in feeding a wolf?

Consider affirmations, which are positive thoughts, as an illustration. I can do my affirmations in the morning.

> I love my team members. We are a high-functioning team built on trust.

Yet throughout the day — the other twenty-three hours and fifty-two seconds — if I am saying:

> Oh my gosh, this team is the worst! If one more person makes an excuse, I am going to scream.

---

**Guess which thought wins!**

---

Finding faults and complaining endlessly without a fix in mind is futile. Whether it is a repeated complaining thought or an expected difficult conversation. Joan of Arc didn't just talk about injustices, she got on her horse and did something about it!

> **Reality Check**
> Dr. Laura Markham reminds us that a complaint is often a way of blaming others, or we blame life – which, of course, is pointless. The best way to address any problem is to begin by accepting the facts of the situation. Then you can begin to take responsibility for making things better.

I am not suggesting you should never complain. In fact, complaining can sometimes lead to positive outcomes-history shows us this through countless examples of social protest. The key is to direct your complaint to someone who can actually help, and to come prepared with facts, evidence, and clear justification.

"So, where do we complain about this?"

For example, we often rely on our elected representatives to fix what's wrong, but they are not all-powerful (nor would we want them to be). In 2009, US Congressman Emanuel Cleaver, II (D., Mo.) got tired of hearing people complain about things that were beyond his ability or available resources to solve, so he introduced a bill that would designate the Wednesday before Thanksgiving as a "Complaint-Free Day." In his resolution, he cited the finding that people complain on average for up to thirty times a day, much of it pointless and even counterproductive.

Cleaver's purpose wasn't to shut off communication with his constituents. Instead, he wanted to emphasize the power of deliberate thinking.

The bill never became law, but the effort is still worth applauding.

> **Reality Check**
> Dr. Travis Bradberry asserts that repeated complaining, in effect, rewires your brain, tending to become your usual response to any situation. And when that's your approach, other people will assume that negativity is basic to your personality.

### Practice Makes Progress

From learning a new language to solo exploration of new lands, mastering something new requires considerable practice time. If you stick with it, the activity can become second nature.

Our communication habits work the same way. Complaining repeatedly, builds the subconscious habit — and even the skill — of complaining.

When martyrs are ruminating on something, they are constantly lodging internal complaints.

### Beware of the Side Effects of Martyr Complaining

Routinely complaining affects both your personality and physical well-being. Think about a time when you complained about something that happened to you. What type of feelings did it evoke in you? The chances are ones that didn't feel too good. There is a biological reason behind this. If you take a moment and focus on a distressing event, your (powerful yet sometimes misused) mind will recreate what happened. Recalling the event requires your brain to synthesize the memory, which causes you to relive the awkward experience and feel the original distress all over again. This is the way our body prepares us for flight or fight. Your brain doesn't know if an event just happened or if it is the same complaint you have been repeating from twenty years ago. Our brain just tries to fill in all of the details of the event.

As you complain, your body releases cortisol, which elevates blood pressure and blood sugar. Cortisol activates your fight-or-flight response. The chemical prompts your body to reroute oxygen, blood, and energy, prioritizing resources needed for immediate survival only. You'll then be set to protect yourself by fleeing or fighting. But, guess what? You are not being chased by a lion. You don't need to have your adrenaline hyped up to protect you from danger in this moment. Consider how many times a day we get triggered.

The excess cortisol generated can harm your immune system. Following that, increased risks include high cholesterol, diabetes, heart disease, obesity, and potentially stroke. I know all of this from firsthand experience.

> **Reality Check**
> Writing in Active Family Magazine, Mark Waldman reports that irritability is like a contagious virus. The emotions in your voice and your face are sensed by every person who meets you, and those effects can affect their neurology.

Complaining and negative thinking can spread from person to person. Just as colds and flu season arrives each winter — and people get vaccinated to protect themselves — unfortunately, there's no vaccine to shield you from the negative effects of MVJs. Did you know complaining and negative thinking can be contagious? Ever hear the term *misery loves company*? Its effect on others is real. Humans possess a mirror neuron system (MNS) that allows us to reflect and absorb the actions and behaviors of those around us.

We learn through spoken or written words, and we also learn through instinctual mimicry.

Learning positive traits through the MNS can make us more empathetic. Ultimately, it comes down to what we observe each day and how attentive we are. We can also pick up toxic behaviors without even thinking.

Complaining and negative thoughts are further shown to impair health, according to medical evidence. Stanford University research shows that negative emotions can harm neurons in the hippocampus, a region of the brain responsible for problem-solving. Good news and bad news — you get to choose between being a problem solver or a complaining martyr.

### Here's the Bad News

If anyone on your team complains constantly, not only will morale suffer, but it may also damage the team's ability to solve problems.

**Heads Up!**

**WE MAY BE OUT OF ANTI-VENOM!**

A moment of mindfulness can be good for your health and those around you. Be aware of which wolf you are feeding with each thought you think.

Another tip for a peaceful mind: Know how to use the word "no."

# HARD TIME SAYING "NO!"

I was working with a large utility company, coaching executives and managers to improve their communication skills.

It quickly became clear why Dawn, one of the managers, was struggling: she found it difficult, if not impossible, to set healthy boundaries for herself. Saying "no" to her employees was nearly unthinkable for her. As a result, Dawn often accepted tasks that other teammates had already handled or could have solved on their own with the help of ChatGPT.

> **Heads Up!**
>
> **MOSQUITO REPELLENT IS MANDATORY!**

Over time, Dawn became the go-to problem solver, at a significant cost to her own well-being.

Dawn ended up doing extra work, eventually confessing to me that her own projects were starting to suffer. She shared stories in our coaching session of her employees' taking advantage of her willingness to help. The truth is that her behavior unintentionally contributed to their laziness.

One of Dawn's employees interrupted our ninety-minute meeting. He needed help to create an Excel document.

**Heads Up!**

**CROCS WON'T EAT YOU UNLESS YOU ARE IN THE WATER WITH THEM**

**"Your Excel skills are much better," he told Dawn, then asked for her help.**

There was an awkward moment when Dawn looked at me for support. Indeed, I could come to her rescue and help her turn him down, but I stayed silent. She hesitated, then sheepishly replied, "Sure."

Once the employee left the room, I spoke with Dawn about the basic skills new hires should have. Sure enough, Excel capability was on the list.

> I wrote a statement for Dawn to say when asked to do the work of others:
>
> **That will not be possible.**

This statement was our starting point. I asked Dawn to say the line out loud. She was tentative and struggled to get the words out. I encouraged her to repeat it, and when she felt ready, I had her record the phrase on her phone. She made multiple recordings.

After each one, we listened, and I gave her feedback. Her confidence and assertiveness were visibly increasing as we carried on with the process. Finally, after fifteen attempts, she nailed it.

After that, we practiced different reactions to workers' demands, like, "I'll help, but this is the last time."

When I checked with Dawn a few months later, she had adopted a dog and was spending her weekends camping off-grid. She was finally experiencing a dream she once assumed was only possible after retiring. Dawn stated that giving her team more autonomy gave her (and a lovely rescue dog) a new lease (or *new leash* as she puts it now) on life.

### Boundaries Build Balance

Martyrs often struggle to set personal boundaries. As noted earlier, much of this behavior traces back to childhood — the origin of every hesitant "no."

Fast forward to the workplace, our increased well-being results from overcoming the internal struggle to say no, creating safe boundaries, and training others how to treat us.

So, how do boundaries benefit you? Boundaries lower burnout, resentment, and stress by safeguarding your emotional, mental, and physical health. They also teach others how to treat you and foster mutual respect in relationships. Boundaries can clarify expectations and reduce misunderstandings. I like to think of boundaries like a channel on a walkie-talkie. Boundaries are a way to create clear communication and reduce static by enforcing a protocol on how we will be treated. Also, walkie-talkies only respond within a certain range.

Creating a technical manual on how others should interact with you starts with reflection on your values, needs, and limits. Boundaries will only work if we know clearly what is acceptable, what is not, and how we anchor them internally.

---

### Setting Boundaries: Six Steps to Protecting Your Habitat

**1. Identify Your Needs**

What makes you feel drained, disrespected, or uneasy? What do you need more of in your life (*e.g.,* rest, space, honesty)?

Example: I feel overwhelmed when I'm expected to respond to work messages after hours. I need time to recharge.

### 2. Acknowledge your limitations.

What are your emotional, physical, and time-related limits? At what point do you find yourself stressed or resentful?

Example: I can't commit to social plans every weekend. I need downtime.

### 3. Define Your Boundaries

What boundaries would help you guard your needs and limits? Be clear and respectful when communicating with it.

For instance: After 6 PM, I will not answer work emails.

### 4. Plan Your Communication

With whom do you need to communicate this boundary? How will you express it calmly and assertively?

Example: I'd like to talk about work hours. I've stopped checking emails after 6 PM to maintain balance.

### 5. Prepare for Pushback

What reactions might you face? How will you stay firm and respectful?

Example: When someone pushes, I reiterate my boundary and propose talking during work time.

### 6. Reflect and Adjust

How did it feel to set the boundary? Did it help? Do you need to adjust it?

Example: I felt nervous but relieved. I might need to remind people a few times.

---

Consistency is crucial for making boundaries stick. Just like learning to get a four-wheel drive out of the mud during monsoon season, success comes from practice- not theory alone.

Boundaries reflect our self-worth. They are the way we teach others how to interact with us. For me, the most striking instance in the wild of that concept was when I watched a single lioness deter a pack of hyenas abide by her boundaries away from her cubs and fresh kill. Her gestures and gaze accomplished all of this. True executive presence if I've ever seen it.

---

### Warning!

Identifying and holding up a mirror to these behaviors won't make you popular. My role model, Charles Darwin, learned that the hard way.

# PLAYING THE SOCIAL SCIENTIST AT THE OFFICE

**After my brief adventure in the Galápagos, I was reminded that people persecuted Darwin for his findings.**

When Darwin touted his conclusions about evolution, prominent scientists scoffed, and the prestigious British Royal Society refused to let him speak.

Scientific methods are uncomplicated. You observe and then capture the facts; and exclude anything from your explanations that isn't necessary. Darwin simply shared what he found. Darwin didn't expect to be rebuked.

Likewise, prepare for mixed or confused reactions when you begin saying "no" more often. This is a new you that others need to process. Because you did not object before, some might see you as difficult or hard to get along with now. Expect discomfort as you create a new normal that includes the word "no." We also have to own up to our part if we've been people-

> **BOOK4U**
>
> Joyce Amy
>
> "Big Bad Boss Tales; Overbearing Management Styles Are All the Rage. Did We Say Rage?"
>
> Washington Post (May 29, 2005)

pleasers. As adults, we can choose to adapt.

Darwin realized that adaptability is essential for evolution. In current times, we like to use the word agile. Try to stay agile and adaptable as you proceed with your boundary plan to ensure your evolution.

---

**My manager responded to my 60 hours of work per week with:**

***"You may have really bad time-management skills."***

---

I can still feel the words cutting through my heart like a knife.

I didn't consider changing my martyr course until my manager asked me why I was spending every weekend in the office.

In the back of this book, you will find self-assessment exercises. Have you noticed any martyr traits in yourself yet? By now, like me, you've probably noticed martyr traits in yourself.

---

**I know I have.**

---

## Three Steps to Martyr Management

### When you identify the Martyr in yourself:

1. To build confidence and reduce guilt, start practicing saying "No" with small requests.
2. Clearly define what you can handle and communicate that. Boundaries are not selfish; they are self-care. Clear expectations mitigate miscommunication.
3. Self-validate: See your own value, not needing others' validation, is liberating.

### When you identify the Martyr in those around you:

1. Politely refuse their task dumping and matching their overwork. Example: *"I appreciate your dedication, and I need to stick to my own priorities right now."*
2. Avoid excessively praising their over-functioning so as not to reward the behavior.
3. Redirect Conversations. If they complain about being overworked, ask what they can delegate or re-prioritize. Example: *"That sounds like a lot — what can you take off your plate?"*

**Key Differentiators**

Office martyrs seek praise for their sacrifices.

Office victims seek pity for their problems.

**Your Next Encounter**

Okay, what about Victims? How do we differentiate between them and martyrs? Let's see!

# FROM MARTYRS TO VICTIMS

**The martyrs and the victims you observe in the workplace might initially seem to have similar personalities.**

Even the best eyes can mistake an unkindness (ravens) for a murder (crows) from afar. To us, it's mistaking a victim for a martyr. In the same way, we sometimes confuse victims with martyrs. Both react poorly to difficulties and misfortune. Martyrs, as shown before, create needless hardship and sorrow for themselves. Victims, on the other hand, may not cause the problems-but they rarely offer solutions.

### Identifying Martyrs and Victims by Their Unique Behaviors

The assessment in the last chapter will help you clarify the line between martyr and victim for your own reflection. Many self-critical responses can apply to either group, but note these important distinctions:

- A victim is hurt *by* something, while a martyr suffers *for* something or someone.
- A victim has something happen to them, while a martyr willingly chooses what happens to them.
- A victim's obituary might say they died *of* something, such as a disease, while a martyr is described by what they died *for*, such as a cause.
- Victims know they are likely to be mistreated before they enter the situation. Martyrs campaign about how unfairly they are being treated but choose to remain in this unfair position.
- Being a victim refers to wounds from the past, while the martyr is defined by the ongoing choice to endure suffering.

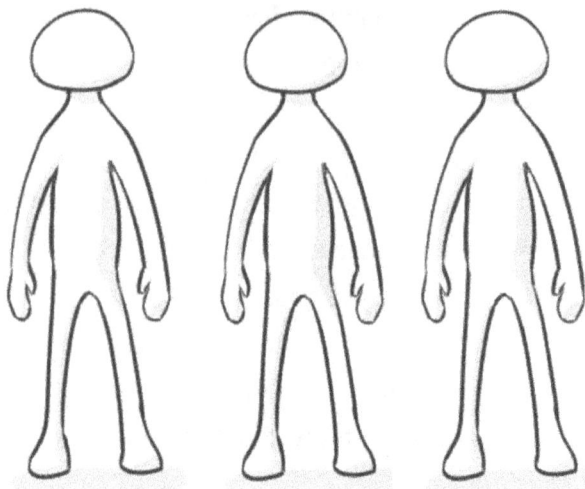

Welcome to the World of Victims! They may be hiding in cubicles or open offices. Beware!

# PART THREE

# VICTIMS

*Cowards die many times before their deaths. The valiant never taste of death but once. Of all the wonders that I yet have heard, it seems to me most strange that men should fear, seeing that death, a necessary end, will come when it will come.*

**- William Shakespeare**
*The Tragedy of Julius Caesar*, Act II, Scene 2

# IDENTIFY THE VICTIM

| | |
|---|---|
| **Behaviors** | The term victim has also been hijacked and transposed onto unsavory characters in the workplace.<br><br>**With our office victims, sympathy is what they seek.** |
| **Key Indicators** | Identifying traits of a victim include:<br><br>• Are quick to blame other people and situations for what does not work in their lives<br>• Become angry at the people or events they think have "done them wrong"<br>• Are self-righteous—they take no personal responsibility for their state<br>• Lack resilience even from minor setbacks<br>• Seem to look for reasons to be upset |
| **Background** | Our phylum of victims (Office Victims) executes their plan differently from the martyr. Our Office Victims possess a toxic personality trait: a "victim mentality" they use to manipulate and shame others. They can take anything and everything personally, giving them extensive sources for their misery.<br><br>Perhaps you have found yourself trapped by a victim, and they moan on as your precious time slips by, time you will never get back. Beware! |
| **Identified** ☐ | Check this box when you feel confident that you have identified a victim, including yourself. |

# THE OFFICE VICTIM

**The examples of victim behavior in this section should help you spot them in the office.**

Like my martyr stories, these are situations that I have learned of, witnessed, or sometimes, lived through.

There have been times I've waved the victim flag, mainly when I felt I'd been mistreated. Have you? Office victims may bring the white flag down to half staff, but they rarely ever bring it down completely.

Victims may already know the considerable benefits their behavior brings. They act out those roles routinely, sometimes out of a lack of self-awareness, and often without the willingness to change.

While any of us can fall into a rut, for victims that rut becomes a way of life.

You'll have opportunities to observe office victims. They might be a colleague, a boss, or even the CEO.

> **Heads Up!**
>
> ALWAYS MAINTAIN A SAFE PERIMETER

**It doesn't matter.**

What they all possess is a toxic personality trait — a victim mentality, which they use to manipulate and shame others at the slightest chance when they feel mistreated or exploited.

---

**Grab those field glasses.**

It's time to sharpen your focus. Let's see some examples.

---

# SAD, SAD SUSAN

**Susan found herself constantly wrapped up in a tragedy, either personal or another's.**

She worried herself sick, convinced that a mole on her arm was cancerous even before her appointment. When the specialist finally gave her the results, it turned out to be nothing serious. Susan's reaction shifted from disbelief to disappointment.

When Susan's life was uneventful, particularly during drama droughts, she'd borrow drama from a friend. She cleverly had fewer than four degrees of separation from almost any tragedy. She wept openly, for instance, over the loss of her dear friend Kate's home. Meanwhile, she had met

Kate only once, when attending a wedding eight years prior. Even though it was Kate's house confirmed to be in the wildfire path, Susan turned the tragedy into her own narrative, fishing for sympathy from everyone.

Though Susan barely knew the victim, she grieved Kate's misfortune as though it were her own, seeking attention and pity through borrowed sorrow.

> **Reality Check**
> **ARE YOU**
> **fr-AGILE?**
> (breakable or flexible)

Whenever Susan looked glum, which was most of the time, her colleagues were reluctant to ask her if she was okay, knowing that a long, dramatic story would ensue.

They even joked that they could watch the news the night before work and guess which tragic situation Susan would add to her woes.

Behind her back, they referred to Susan as "Debbie Downer," which usually followed up with the mock sound effect that went something like, "Wha, wha, whaaaa."

---

**Susan discovered early in life that sympathy was a kind of attention.**

---

As a child, when she suffered from a scraped knee or the passing of her grandmother, it was the only time she felt she was getting undivided attention. As an adult, it did not matter if it was her own suffering or another's. Whether it was her own pain or someone else's, she constantly craved the attention it brought.

---

**Your Next Encounter**

Let me introduce you to another victim, a coworker named Danielle.

# IT'S A FAMILY TRADITION

**Danielle worked in data processing at a Fortune 100 company. After three years, a management position opened.**

The promotion would go to either Danielle or her colleague Ingrid. When Danielle was told of Ingrid receiving the position, she complained to the hiring manager, "If you had given me the same support you gave Ingrid, I would have been getting that promotion. You pick favorites, and I guess that's how it goes."

Flashback fifteen years earlier, Danielle hid at the top of the stairs, covering her ears while she listened to her father's rant, "The manager always gives the warm buyers to his brother-in-law."

Her father was a used car salesman. When business was good and luck was shining on them, the family would move to a new house for a fresh start.

# IT'S A FAMILY TRADITION

When money wasn't coming in, and there wasn't enough for rent, they would flee in the middle of the night, taking what their old car could carry and leaving behind a massive rent bill along with the rest of their possessions.

As she sat at the top of the stairs, Danielle knew she would soon have to pick her favorite things for the midnight exodus.

Conditioned early in life, Danielle came to believe the world was unfair, and most circumstances were out of her control. While we can have empathy for young Danielle, grown Danielle needs to learn a new way of being.

### Your Next Encounter

Let's look at an example where someone made a choice not to wear the victim hat.

# RIP FOR THE RFP

**The RFP (request for proposal) was due at midnight.**

We're discussing a situation where millions of dollars were on the line. Because a winning response to a request for proposal (RFP) requires volumes of narratives and data, writing it overnight is impossible. Submitting bids past the deadline is not an option. If you miss the deadline even by a minute, the committee disqualifies your bid.

John, along with his team of three, had spent a month working on their company's RFP. They invested countless hours in the research, design, and documentation of their solution. This one deal alone was worth $8 million over the next three years. Their company was a leading candidate for the win because market data revealed their solution best met the RFP needs. Their boss reminded them frequently, "This is ours to lose."

Gathered around John's computer, the team merged their work and finished the documents. With only thirty minutes until the midnight deadline, John felt confident that they would make it. The legal team and senior management completed, reviewed, and endorsed the document. The last step involved uploading the file to an email and sending it.

John sat back with pride and declared:

**"Great job, team! With a half-hour to spare!"**

But as if the universe was in the mood for some dark humor, John's computer screen went not black but blue! If you've ever witnessed the "blue screen of death," you know the sinking feeling as the reality sets in the hard drive has just crashed.

Like EMT's rushing into action, John's team performed the perfunctory reboot. No luck. At 11:48 p.m. that tragic evening, they pronounced John's computer deceased. And because they'd been working furiously right up to the deadline, the nightly backup of John's computer had not yet taken place.

Because they had no way to recover the files and no time to put the RFP back together again, they waved the white flag.

Now, put yourself in John's shoes. Do you think John could have considered himself a victim? Sure. Would John expect his boss to console him while he shared every detail of the failed submission? Probably not.

Recall that victims accept their suffering. What they don't do is take responsibility for dealing with the causes of their misfortune.

**Reality Check**

People tend to use **AGILE** to mean **FAST** and **FLEXIBLE**

But in project management the technical definition of **AGILE** is **EXPERIMENTAL** and possibly **DISPOSABLE** if it doesn't work

Could John have done anything else differently to mitigate this tragedy? Of course, and that's exactly what he did the next morning. In the first email he sent out the next day, he took responsibility of what happened and proposed a new system for backing up any work in progress.

But if John had chosen the victim role, he might have spent the night asking, "Why, why did this happen to me?"

He could have gone into the office the next day with excuses such as the injustice of being given an unreliable computer to perform such an important task.

Losing a significant bid is painful, but it happens. Unlike a victim, John felt the pain but moved on.

Deadlines and the overwork to meet them cause stress, but so can a slack work schedule and the accompanying rumors of layoffs.

# RUMORS OF LAYOFFS

**They announced a competitor would acquire the organization. After the acquisition, staff members assumed layoffs would soon follow.**

Consumed by the worst possible situations, Andre fell into a "what-if" mindset: "What if I lose my job? What if I lose my house with no money to pay the mortgage? What if I lose everything?"

While his colleagues focused on discussing options, Andre was busy with what-iffing. But there was not yet any need for worry. Andre didn't even know if he would be a part of the layoffs — or if there even would be layoffs!

On the other side of the same cubicle wall, after hours of fretting about the possible layoffs, a different emotion kicked in for Willow. She told herself:

> **Heads Up!**
>
> REMEMBER TO STAY HYDRATED

*"Nobody has worked harder here than I have. I can't believe this is how I get thanked after eighteen years of service. This is BS!"*

Andre and Willow had comparable years of service, skill sets, job levels, and pay rates. Their adjoining cubicles were identical, but their reactions to the rumors could not have been more different.

Andre persisted in victim behavior.

Willow took a deep breath and determined that this was the wake-up call she needed to start her own graphic design company.

Willow resolved that — layoff or no layoff — there would be no downside to the downsize for her.

If you have identified the victim potential in yourself or someone you know, understand that undergoing a setback doesn't make you a victim.

No, you win the victim badge by dwelling on the experience, reinforcing feelings of disappointment or defeat, and doing little to mitigate or prevent the situation.

Perhaps you know someone who is still ruminating over an unfairness that happened three decades ago.

## Your Next Encounter

Many of us have recently felt like victims during the worldwide pandemic.

# THE COVID EXPERIENCE

**Have you had a moment in the past few years when you felt like a victim?**

Possibly it happened when the world locked down because of the pandemic, facing the unknown.

Together we stumbled through the fear, confusion, and grief of the Covid experience. Think about the people you know- how differently did they cope as the months stretched into years?

Now reflect on yourself. Did you ever yield to your inner victim because it felt like the only option available? If so, that's okay. We forgive ourselves and gain wisdom from experience.

Looking back, what made you get up the next day and keep trying?

Life presents difficulties for all of us, without exception. We try to dig deep, dust ourselves off, and get back into the game of life. It takes deep courage to be resilient.

Most of the world got kicked pretty hard starting in 2020.

Give yourself credit for making it through — and recognize that you have developed some coping skills along the way.

> **Fun Fact**
>
> **A WATER BUFFALO IS GENTLE AS A MILK COW**
>
> *not!*

# MADISON AND HANNA

**Madison hoped to lead a high-profile project; however, Hanna was selected instead.**

Choosing victimhood, Madison refused to support Hanna when team issues arose. He claimed he didn't care if the team succeeded and admitted he didn't want Hanna to get credit.

Instead of contributing, Madison wasted his energy plotting to sabotage Hanna. By giving himself permission to act this way, he leaned into negativity. Victim behavior can result from notions of entitlement and selfishness. Victims may feel they have been seriously wronged in their lives, just like Madman Madison, and the world owes them a payback.

Feeling entitled to success can easily lead to selfish behavior.

In short, victims often believe they've suffered enough already, and it's their turn to prosper. Note that this attitude stems from being resigned to fate, requiring no positive action on the victim's part.

**Reality Check**

Have you ever thought,

*If I can't have it, neither can you!*

Identifying the victim in ourselves and others requires deep observation and connecting data points It's also important to rule out imposter syndrome in this analysis.

> **Reality Check**
> A research study conducted by Stanford University and published in the Journal of Personality and Social Psychology found that feeling wronged leads to a sense of entitlement and selfish behavior.

# IMPOSTORS

I started noticing impostor syndrome in my consulting work a few years back.

The first time I was introduced to the term, my immediate thought was, *Don't we all experience self-doubt?* A therapist shared with me that there is a difference between having a moment of doubt and having a *mindset* of default doubt. While a moment passes, a mindset predicts. Impostor syndrome is the latter, a predictive mindset.

I mention impostor syndrome in this discussion of victims because a lack of self-confidence is usually at the heart of this behavior. However, persistent, unchecked feelings of inadequacy can also afflict martyrs and even jerk personalities.

> **Reality Check**
> According to neuroscientist Marwa Azab, PhD, impostors will doubt their abilities even when there is evidence they've actually performed well. They may regard success as a matter of luck. Feeling oneself to be a fraud can lead to anxiety, fear of exposure, and overwork.

This may surprise you, but impostor syndrome is not considered a psychological disorder. The *Diagnostic and Statistical Manual of Mental Disorders* (DSM), used by healthcare professionals to diagnose psychological syndromes and disorders, does not list it. (Professionals may instead refer to imposter phenomenon or imposter feelings.)

When self-doubt becomes constant, the follow-up question is: Do you want to change it? If you answer yes, I invite you to pay closer attention to your words or thoughts. Should it be someone in your life experiencing impostor syndrome, be attentive if you hear them mentioning any of:

- Everyone here is so much better than I am. I'm a fake.
- My manager will discover I am a fraud.
- I was just lucky to get into a good school and get good grades. Maybe my luck is going to run out.
- It is all going to catch up with me, then everyone will know.

It's devastating to witness a skilled, dedicated professional doubt themselves, especially when less competent colleagues succeed through politics.

In the next chapter, which concludes this survey of victim behavior, I'll offer coping skills for dealing with impostor syndrome — whether in yourself or someone else.

### Managing Impostor Syndrome

Again, impostor syndrome can affect anyone, especially our MVJs. Self-doubt fuels this behavior, and even the strongest people can panic when it strikes. I'll share coping skills I've refined and successfully used with clients over the years.

Keep in mind that early life experiences manifest in adulthood while identifying MVJ behaviors. If you are facing impostor syndrome, take a moment to consider what the first seven years of your life were like for you. I often notice a subtle connection between my clients' present behavior and qualities, both good and bad, they've carried forward from childhood.

For instance, a strong work ethic could've helped you achieve recognition and success. Great! But what if your devoted work ethic results from constantly trying to prove yourself? A sign of impostor syndrome may involve a lack of acknowledging achievements.

I understand that finding solace at work is beneficial. But I invite you to consider this: has it quietly become your entire identity?

Given your demonstrated competence, why the constant self-doubt?

If only we had a time machine to tell our younger selves:

**"It's okay. I'm enough!"**

We can't go back and reprogram our past, but we can reshape our beliefs starting today.

---

> For more support, please read *Find Peace on Purpose* by Giulia Cappelli, which I also mentioned earlier.

---

In my coaching practice, I've developed some exercises to help people shift from an impostor mindset to one of owning their success.

# MANAGE YOUR MINDSET

**Thirty Days for Three Minutes (30:3) Challenge**

The first technique involves brief daily journaling for one month.

When I began working with a sales team, their numbers reflected a victim mentality. For thirty-two consecutive months, their sales results followed the 80/20 rule: Most of them (80 percent of the team) generated only 20 percent of the sales.

> **BOOK4U**
>
> Gallup,
>
> *"Performance Measures That Motivate Employees"*
>
> (2017)

After conducting one-on-one assessments, peer-reviewed interviews, and self-doubt confessions, I came to suspect that the team's disappointing history had turned into a self-fulfilling prophecy. Most relied on a few top performers and felt they could never keep up. Meanwhile, the lower performers likely carried an extra burden of guilt.

They feared they didn't deserve credit for it even when the team's results were good. I challenged myself to find a system where we could install an upgraded sense of confidence in each of the team members. After all, they were already successful at some point in their career, or they wouldn't have been hired for their current role.

### Step 1: Capture Your Experience

Here's the exercise I had each member of the team undertake. You will need the following items:

- Timer (on your phone)
- Notebook or journal
- Pen

**Aim:** To deepen the neural pathways of confidence.

**Process.** In your journal, revisit your past successes and the challenges you have already overcome. Write them down, reflect on them, and allow yourself to recognize your capability.

**Set a timer for three minutes in every daily session.**

Talk about a challenge you overcame or a success you had back then. Here's a tip: *Write in the third person.* Tell your story as if someone else is sharing it. This approach can help you be more objective in your later evaluations.

For example:

*Stevie is a real champion! Balancing full-time work, raising two toddlers, and finishing her degree was a challenging feat she accomplished. Imagine the fortitude and time management skills it took to achieve such a feat.*

Continue writing until the three-minute alarm rings. Do this activity religiously for thirty days. Start again from day one if you skip a day!

### Step 2: Evaluate Your Achievements

When you review your journal, reflect on your achievements in terms of both quantity and quality:

- What did you overcome?
- How did you make it through the tough times?
- Are you celebrating your achievements or just moving on without enough reflection?

After the sales team took the 30:3 challenge, I conducted one-on-one coaching to encourage their positive progress. The results were observable shifts in the sales team's overall feelings — from impostors to confident achievers.

The benefits I saw from the sales team included:

- They were bolder and took more initiative. They made more cold calls.
- They showed greater confidence in booking meetings with prospects.
- They asked more closing questions, thereby finalizing more deals.

### Step 3: Upping Your Game

Take this activity to the next level by slightly changing the perspective. Write in first person for the next month. For example:

> *I am so proud of how far I have come. Becoming a college graduate was not something I was expected to do. Look at me. I am among the first in the family to have a degree. I am a strong role model for my kids. I'm confident I can achieve anything I focus on.*

By recounting our successes, we are training the brain to move beyond imposter feelings and embrace confidence.

### Reframe Your Thoughts

Here is another way to adopt a more confident mindset.

Have you heard of the *reticular activating system?* This brain region handles your safety. The image that comes to mind for me is Spider-Man's web. When you make a statement, your brain searches for ways to back it up or, like Spider-Man, casts a web.

You've likely experienced the reticular activating system without realizing it. For example, you might think, "I want to plan a safari." Suddenly, it feels like African safaris are everywhere—friends are talking about them, travel ads pop up online, and even the Showcase Showdown on The Price Is Right features an African safari.

When my friend decided to purchase a new red Honda Accord, she called to report that she had started seeing them everywhere

— in the parking lot, on the freeway, and even advertised during the evening news. I didn't want to tell her they were always there, she just activated the part of the brain that made them obvious to her.

But this function doesn't always work to your advantage. It doesn't matter if your thought benefits you or not. It will simply cast a net to support whatever you say.

For instance, "It will be a great day today," prompts your reticular activating system to seek evidence to support that belief.

Despite the rain forecast, some people optimistically say, "It will be a great day today." Those folks come from an optimistic mindset.

They are cultivating positive thinking habits. These are the same people who proclaim their long commute is a terrific way to get caught up on their podcast list. Their reticular activating system will continue to look for positive attributes during the commute on that rainy day. They're the ones who always find the silver lining.

Now picture waking up, hitting your toe, and yelling, "This is a rainy day from hell!" without noticing the irony. This will be the day you get a flat tire; your coupon is expired, and your phone battery won't hold a charge.

My challenge to you is to be aware of your thoughts and pay particular attention to which thoughts are not serving you. Impostor syndrome can spin you into a prolonged state of bad luck.

Following the examples below, reframe your thoughts to ensure positive outcomes.

| If you are tempted to say: | Reframe the thought as: |
| --- | --- |
| They are going to find out I am a phony. | My skills speak for themselves, like when I (insert achievement). |
| I haven't rehearsed enough. My presentation is going to be awful. | No one is more knowledgeable about this information or cares more than I do. I am the person who will deliver this information persuasively. |

I'm not suggesting you put a happy sticker on your phone when the battery is dead! No, I am suggesting you develop a mindset that leans toward affirmative curiosity rather than rigid negativity.

We encounter ample times in life to hone our crisis-management skills. Questioning whether we are good enough should not take our valuable energy.

Don't worry — you will have plenty of opportunities to put these new skills into practice. In the next chapter, we will explore the difficult individuals in our lives.

---

**Your Next Encounter**

Let's see if we can practice establishing and reinforcing a positive mindset as we enter the world of jerks.

---

## VICTIMS' DILEMMA — DEALING WITH A JERK

**If you're bullied, your coping strategy may be to put yourself in the role of martyr or victim voluntarily.**

By now, it won't surprise you that martyrs tend to endure being bullied — sometimes even acting proud of being a sidekick — while victims conclude they were simply born under an unlucky sign.

You may ask yourself why someone would stay in a position if bullied. From what I've witnessed, it comes down to:

- Fear of loss of income
- Worry that a new job would be challenging to secure
- Hope that the few years until their retirement will pass quickly
- Deep passion for the job or a belief they are making a difference

### Janette's Slippery Slide

I met Janette around the time I began working for a privately held billion-dollar company. She was dynamic, engaged, and passionate about her position as a project manager. From our very first meeting, I thought Janette would be an ideal employee.

But I noticed a change in Janette when the stock market crashed in 2008, and the country was heading into a recession. It was a period filled with great worry and fear. Even financial analysts couldn't predict how long or brutal this banking collapse would be.

This marked the start of widespread layoffs across the business landscape. The managers' motto was: Do more with less! Employees were now juggling two, three, or even four roles. The looming threat of job loss fueled a silent pressure: Just shut up and do your job! I specifically remember hearing a manager at a client site threaten staff with:

**"There are fifteen people lined up for your job."**

Two of Janette's colleagues were let go, and she lived in constant fear that she would be next. At the same time, her husband was injured at work and became unemployed. With four children, the family told themselves they could handle an accident or an illness- because Janette's company offered excellent health insurance. But she knew she'd lose that safety net if she were downsized.

I coached Janette through the days, weeks, and months before the economy recovered. When the business engine was churning again, companies that had downsized learned a big lesson: Over the short term, it is possible to extract more productivity from workers if you let them know they can replace them. The do-more-with-less mindset helped some companies become more profitable than ever after the recession. Executives and shareholders collected large bonuses and became the big winners- a "new normal" had begun.

> **Heads Up!**
>
> **KEEP BINOCULAR LENSES CLEAR**

But that wasn't the end of the story. As the economy improved, unemployment rates decreased, opportunities increased, and employees left for better jobs. Employers soon learned that replacing seasoned workers with new hires wasn't easy. The younger staff needed specific training beyond their academics, and until they got it, the quality of products and customer service suffered.

Just as you must stay alert in the jungle or risk missing the lion about to pounce, complacency carried its own dangers. That's exactly what happened to Janette.

Janette's group got to know their new VP of operations, a no-nonsense man named Ken, whose first act was stunning: he terminated every employee and required each of them to convince him why they should be hired back.

It was a rude awakening, and Janette had to prove her worth all over again.

I coached Janette through her presentation. The years of stress showed on her face as she practiced it. Out of nowhere, she burst into tears and asked me:

> **"Who will hire me if I don't get my job back? I'm almost sixty. I haven't updated my skills, and everyone else who was let go is still looking for a job."**

In Janette's mind, her ability to secure another position was so limited she was willing to live with the daily fear and intimidation of being let go.

She'd tolerated verbal abuse, mood swings, and sabotage from her manager, who held back praise, criticized her continually, and appeared to be setting her up for failure.

Janette was a top performer who let herself fall down the slippery slide to victimhood. She could have stayed in that state of mind until her retirement, reflecting mainly on her disappointments and hardly ever giving herself credit for her career achievements.

Janette won her job back, mainly because the termination was simply an intimidation tactic. I cautioned her that — even though she felt fortunate to return to the same old grind — she'd be healthier and saner if she could set some boundaries.

### Your Next Encounter

Rather than tell you how Janette climbed back up the hill of self-esteem, I'll say that she followed the advice I gave her — which I offer to you in the next chapter.

## WHEN YOU FEEL LIKE A VICTIM

**As sure as a jackal will scavenge remains from a hyena, dreadful things will happen in life.**

You've probably felt life has treated you unfairly. Feeling like a victim occasionally is standard for anyone. The difference between feeling like a victim and becoming one is the time you spend camping in the backcountry of victimhood.

Everyone has a way of dealing with obstacles. When faced with a challenge or a setback, a person with a victim mentality defaults to *poor me mode* (PMM). When trapped in PMM, victims cannot find a solution. They are too far into their dark tunnel. Their perspective only allows them to continue seeing insurmountable challenges. PMM becomes a self-fulfilling prophecy: They perceive the light at the end of the tunnel as a speeding train headed straight toward them.

# WHEN YOU FEEL LIKE A VICTIM

> **BOOK4U**
>
> Jerry Cianciolo,
>
> "A Substitute for 'Complaint Free Wednesday,'"
>
> Wall Street Journal, Eastern Edition (November 21, 2017)

The victim is rarely at a loss for words when sharing something sour they have experienced.

The pathway out of the tunnel of victimhood takes deliberate steps. Now, I'm not saying it's easy. Until you muster the courage, your feet may feel loaded with lead weights. The coaching might seem too simple, but it works if you persist.

## SIX STEPS TO EMPOWERMENT

1. Name the incident and circumstances that made you feel like a victim.
2. When that feeling occurs again, ask yourself whether this is becoming a habit and, ultimately, a recurring mindset.
3. Ask yourself what benefit this negative mindset gives you.
4. Reframe your thoughts. Begin each day with statements that affirm beneficial outcomes.
5. Some of your complaints will be legitimate. Address those complaints only to a person who has the power to resolve them.
6. Understand that, often, the person who has the most power to solve a problem is yourself. Take action!

### And If It's Not Just You

Have you already identified a victim? If so, support them without enabling them. Fair warning, you may quickly become an amateur therapist doing free work.

It usually starts innocuously, perhaps when the victim simply asks, "How are you?" To which you reply, "Fine. And you?"

Just to spend half an hour hearing unwanted details about their gingivitis. I'm not referring to the top five most stressful life events, such as the death of a loved one, divorce, relocation, serious illness or injury, or losing your job.

Each of those major life events requires a healing process, frequently with the help of professionals.

We'll be concentrating on daily occurrences in this conversation, looking at why some people surmount challenges and others get bogged down. It's important to realize that the events may be unimportant or even insignificant. However, continually becoming upset by anything that goes wrong will become a severe condition that will impair your work performance and personal relationships.

Remember the famous quote by the Japanese writer Haruki Murakami: "Pain is inevitable, but suffering is optional." Make a mental memorandum to repeat these words to yourself as often as necessary to stay grounded. Use this principle as a starting point to gain command of your life.

> **Reality Check**
> "Pain is inevitable. Suffering is optional."
> - Haruki Murakami

Also, if you realize you're being a jerk because you feel victimized, you can acknowledge the behavior and choose a better approach.

When dealing with a jerk, victims should experiment with different strategies to find what's effective. The animal kingdom provides a valuable lesson, well-illustrated by the gopher snake. A gopher snake can mimic the actions of a rattlesnake so well that it scares off potential predators. Perhaps this lesson can help you train a jerk in a new way to treat you!

In the next part of the book, I'll help you identify jerks and their tricks. You may find your own way to shake the rattle to deter these menaces.

### Three Steps to Victim Management

When you identify the victim in yourself:

**1. Pause and Reflect**

Ask yourself:

- What exactly am I feeling — frustrated, overlooked, disrespected?
- What story am I telling myself about this situation?
- Is there any part of this I *can* influence?

### 2. Shift from Blame to Ownership

Acts, even small ones — like documenting your work or clarifying expectations — can restore your feeling of control. Instead of focusing on what others are doing *to* you, ask:

- What can I do differently?
- What support do I need to ask for?

### 3. Practice Self-Compassion

Feeling like a victim doesn't make you weak — it means you're human. Be kind to yourself, but don't stay stuck there.

**When you identify the victim in those around you:**

### 1. Acknowledge Their Feelings

Show empathy without reinforcing the victim narrative.
**Example:** *"That sounds frustrating. What do you think would help?"*

### 2. Shift the Focus to Solutions

Gently redirect it from complaints to action.
**Example:** *What's one thing you could do to improve the situation?"*

### 3. Avoid Enabling

Don't jump in to fix everything for them. Let them take ownership of their role in the problem — and the solution.

## 94 MARTYRS, VICTIMS AND JERKS

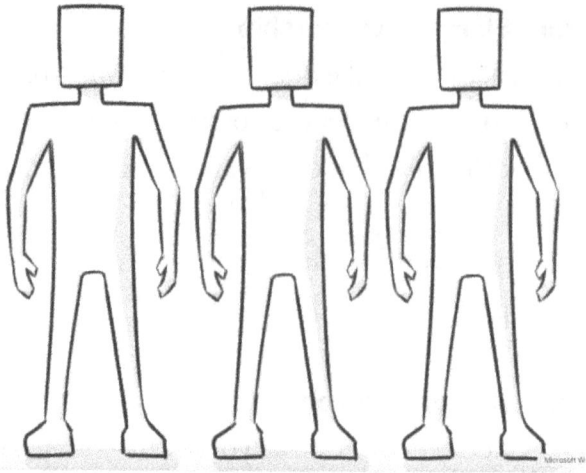

Welcome to the World of Jerks! Have you ever been one? Are you now? Or are you suffering under the claws of another?

# PART FOUR

# JERKS

**What did the lion say to the gazelle?**

*"Nice to eat you."*

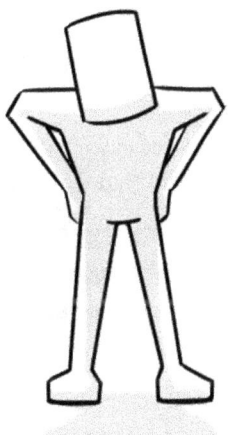

| | |
|---|---|
| **IDENTIFY THE JERK** | |
| **Behaviors** | You can easily find jerks in most ecosystems. They are the simplest to spot as they are rarely concerned with providing camouflage for their intentions.<br><br>**With our office jerks, their behavior is a thinly veiled means to garner power.** |
| **Key Indicators** | You can identify a jerk by:<br><br>• Seeing them bully others<br>• They reject an idea before the speaker delivers it fully<br>• A lack of respect for personal space<br>• A lack of care of how their words and actions affect those around them |
| **Background** | It's all about power—not only as a point of pride but also to control others. With little regard for the impact on the environment, they kick down while cheerfully climbing the corporate ladder.<br><br>The population of jerks in the workplace seems to increase at a rate that jeopardizes the habitat. |
| **Identified** ☐ | Check this box when you feel confident that you have identified a jerk, including yourself. |

## WHAT ABOUT THIS BOOK GRABBED YOU?

**This part of the book investigates the most disruptive of the MVJ trilogy.**

It wouldn't surprise or offend me if you skipped the first few chapters and jumped right to this part on jerks.

In a poll, I asked groups which of the three types they found most disruptive: martyrs, victims, or jerks. Many answered "jerks," and confirmed that their experiences with them had profoundly affected their lives and workplaces.

With a heavy heart, I share stories of workplace suffering — my own and others.

I am deeply grateful to the courageous individuals who shared their stories. Your bravery in reclaiming your power is inspiring. While your identities remain confidential, may your stories serve as a beacon of hope.

In the following chapters, we will explore the various jerks you might encounter at work.

From peer to boss, I have stories highlighting the effects of jerks' behavior on those around them. You're encouraged to calculate how these negative behaviors impact your organization's profits through turnover or lawsuits.

> **Heads Up!**
>
> PITH HELMETS MAY LOOK SILLY BUT YOU WILL BE GLAD YOU WORE YOURS

If you were bullied as a child or have worked alongside a jerk, please consider this a trigger warning. The stories may dredge up memories.

Conversely, if the jerk in my narrative sounds a little like you, congratulations on your awareness! Spoiler alert: We all show up a little jerky at some point. So yes, we will also turn the lenses on ourselves.

### Jerk Spotting

Binoculars in hand, let's see if we can identify the most notorious of the Big Three in their natural habitat of the workplace.

Our definition of the Jerk is someone who is rude, dismissive, aggressive, or consistently undermines others. This definition casts a wide net, making it easy to classify a range of behaviors- and people- as jerk-like.

We have plenty of examples to consider when we think about jerks, as they have existed for ages. Consider the outdated cartoon trope of a knuckle-dragging cave dweller looking for a bride, who then knocks the unsuspecting prey over the head with a club and drags her back to his lair. However, it's important to note that not all jerks are men. In my consulting work, I've encountered my share of XX-chromosome jerks as well.

Since the rise of #MeToo, jerks have been in the news, their secrets exposed and can no longer hide in corporate America. Familiar names of celebrities, politicians, and CEOs as perpetrators of harassment, assault, or other misconduct allegations have emerged.

In the past, under a more direct workplace model, the boss was like a ship's captain, whether the seas were calm or stormy. Teams might have grumbled in private, but no one risked speaking up. Tolerating a manager's misconduct was often considered an occupational norm. After all, you didn't want to rock the captain's boat- because doing so meant you might be thrown overboard. *Until now.*

> **Reality Check**
> This 2014 book title almost says it all:
> *The Narcissist Next Door: Understanding the Monster in Your Family, in Your Office, in Your Bed – in Your World*
>     - by Jeffrey Kluger (Riverhead Books/Penguin Putnam).

You probably encountered some unpleasant kids on the playground growing up, and chances are, you've met just as many, if not more, in the workplace. Yes, jerks are prevalent in business. Why is that? Perhaps because they assume intimidation gets results. They get what they want. But, long term, often at a high cost. Deadlines might be met or sales quotas exceeded. Long-term metrics show that the behavior of jerks negatively affects the team and the company. If low morale and high employee turnover are frequent occurrences because of a single individual's behavior, it signifies a fundamental issue within the corporate culture that demands attention.

Unfortunately, most jerk bosses get away with their intimidating practices, at least for a time — until senior management or shareholders see the consequences, or some brave employee calls them out.

Whether they are trying to dominate the playground or the weekly meeting, they all share one common trait.

**Can you guess what that is?**

# JERKS ARE BULLIES

**Yes, that's it. All jerks threaten others in some fearful way.**

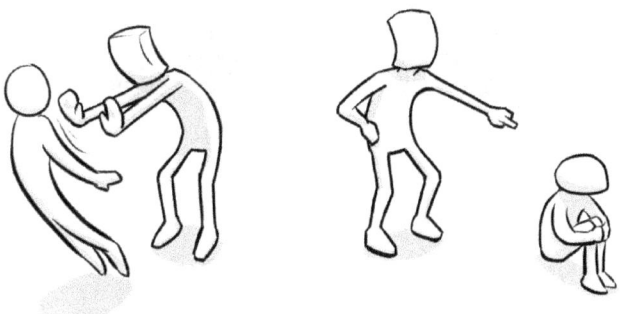

Bullying is something I understand well. On the playground, kids shoved others aside to be first to the top of the slide. They leaped off the teeter-totter when their less weighty schoolmate was high in the air. As these kids grew older, those same aggressive behaviors began showing up in the workplace. The games of recess turned into battles for leadership, recognition, and prominence.

In 2017 (released again in the 2021 survey), a national study conducted by the Workplace Bullying Institute stated that bullying can take the form of mistreatment, threats, humiliation, intimidation, sabotage, or verbal abuse.

> **BOOK4U**
>
> *Workplace Bullying Institute,*
>
> *"2021 Workplace Bullying Statistics Report,"*
>
> *(January, 2024)*

The source of the abuse might be a single coworker or even several working together. When jerks gain power over others, they often dominate their teams. Martyrs and victims may join forces with the jerk to gain favor or because they lack the courage to resist. In some cases, terrible people simply back other terrible people.

Managers of jerks might celebrate their early successes, but eventually, the repercussions always surface.

---

**Your Next Encounter**

Against this background, I'll paint a picture of a classic jerk I spotted in the wild. See how much he resembles someone you know.

---

# KEVIN THE BULLY

**Everything was fine until one eventful Monday morning.**

My customer called to share that they were reviewing their vendor list. They were asking for proposals for all current contracts. Regardless of the success of our projects, we needed to resubmit our offerings for approval.

Surprised and concerned, I called my internal champion to find out why this was happening.

My champion told me that, the previous Friday, our customer's new VP of operations had dropped the hatchet and laid off half the team. The remaining team was required to reapply for their positions. (Yes, this is the same case I cited previously about Janette. But there's more to tell here.)

Bidders and potential rivals learned price was the initial evaluation point, with quality second. So, all those years I'd spent raising the bar on quality might not guarantee a win. Not to sound like a victim, of course.

Likewise, my efforts at making the director and managers look like heroes might be useless. This would be a cold game of metrics — dollars first, then some objective features and benefits.

> **Heads Up!**
>
> **YOUR GUIDE MAY SOMETIMES SHOUT IN SWAHILI SO AS NOT TO HURT YOUR FEELINGS**

My contact, who developed into a friend over the years, shared the new world order with me as I planned my strategy. My plan was to maintain the initial price and provide more flexibility in scheduling and cancelations.

I was hoping our client would leverage this time to eliminate poor vendors and keep only reliable ones. With fewer vendors around, we could grab a larger share, and the increased sales could help maintain low prices.

Excited to be on the shortlist of vendors, I worked tirelessly on the proposal, jumping through every hoop to meet the requirements.

After six long weeks of waiting, the final vendor list was announced, and yes, we made the shortlist. Time to celebrate! But the celebration was short-lived. The very next day, I received a call from Patrice, the coordinator for the director with whom I would be working.

From the beginning, the previous director, Ian, and I developed a deep respect for each other and a trusting relationship. Our working relationship produced incredible results and fostered a sense of creativity and fun.

The adage is still true: you don't know what you have until it's gone!

Patrice scheduled the Skype call, warning me that her boss, Kevin, did not tolerate tardiness, and said she'd email me the talking points. It was already 5 p.m. and with our call scheduled for the next morning; I knew it would be a long night.

> **BOOK4U**
>
> Robert Killoren,
>
> "The Toll of Workplace Bullying,"
>
> Research Management Review (Vol. 20, No. 1, 2014)

Looking back, the more thoughtful manager I am today would have pushed back- rescheduling the call for two days later to allow proper preparation. Unfortunately, at the time, I agreed to the unbalanced arrangement, frantically weighing what in my personal life I'd need to cancel that night to make time.

It was 1:00 a.m. when I finally saved my last file to present to Kevin and closed my laptop. After a few hours of sleep, I started planning for Kevin's first impression of me. I jumped on the call early to ensure the online meeting link worked. Minutes passed, then a quarter-hour, and still no Kevin. He finally jumped on the call twenty minutes late, with no apologies and only a curt introduction.

I knew right away that working with Kevin would differ significantly from my experience with Ian.

I believed I had no choice but to endure the abuse because my livelihood and that of my team depended on those checks getting signed.

---

> To let you in on my mindset: I thought I had no choice but to allow myself to be treated unfairly. #victim

---

Over the next year, I got used to Kevin's impatience, arrogance, and reluctance to give praise. During that time, I racked up six big successes that made Kevin look like a hero. At this point, I have been with this company, serving this customer, for seven years, with a 100 percent record of meeting expectations.

### Pleasing Ungrateful Kevin

It was a Friday afternoon, and Kevin called me to ask for help with a project. Remarkably, he had called me directly and didn't schedule through his admin. He asked me to put together a briefing, saying he wouldn't have time to do it over the next week. Compared to all the intense projects we had already pulled off, this task was easy for me. I asked him a series of questions and to clarify his goals. I was confident I'd be able to deliver exactly the presentation he needed.

When he hung up, I took a deep breath and thought:

---

*I am finally a trusted advisor. This is a fork in the road.* How wrong I was!

---

Based on his agreed-upon requirements, I developed the briefing and emailed it to him. Several days turned into a week, and I still had not heard feedback from him. As I was pondering whether to call him, Patrice called me. Her first words were, "Do not get upset."

That's a terrible way to begin a conversation. Brain science says that kind of warning will backfire. Then, I started stressing about why I might get upset.

I sighed deeply, then just said, "Okay."

She continued, "Jen, I just had to let you know that, over the past week, Kevin has been bashing the briefing you put together for him. He brought it up at least twice just today. I thought you should know so you could conduct damage control."

I felt totally crushed because of a couple of things. First, I fretted he did not value our relationship enough to call me and share his feelings. Second, I was honestly shocked the project was so wrong after he approved the requirements.

With this inside information, I emailed Kevin to salvage the project. I was careful not to hint that Patrice had tipped me off.

The next day on my follow-up call, he tried to deflect his annoyance through humor. But in jest, there can be truth. As though it was a trivial matter, he quips, "I didn't know what that was you sent me."

> **BOOK4U**
>
> Lisa Belkin,
>
> "Working for a Boss Who Bullies,"
>
> New York Times, Late Edition East Coast (May 8, 2005)

But I knew from Patrice's heads-up that he was angry. We talked through the message points of his presentation, and it became clear he'd changed the requirements and not shared them with me.

Nothing I could have produced based on his initial instructions would have hit the mark because he'd moved the target.

> **Heads Up!**
>
> **DO NOT FEED THE FOWL**

I work diligently with my clients to ensure an authentic exchange. I'm no stranger to difficult feedback. I expect fairness, and in new working relationships, we learn the dance of "create and edit." They require a response, want revisions, so I edit and they OK it. We iterate until we agree we've got it right.

Even though I had worked hard all those years and had a perfect track record, Kevin continued to micromanage me and question each step I took on projects.

My resentment built up, and feelings of self-doubt crept in.

While Kevin wasn't a blatant bully, he used his authority to create discomfort and intimidation. He was disarming as a bully because he talked with a sweet voice and had an enticing Irish accent.

But his sarcasm could cut you to the bone, and there was often viciousness behind his smile.

In a later chapter on jerks, I will tell you what I did to keep Kevin from wearing me down. It works still to this day!

But next, I want to discuss how a bully's intimidation affects the efficiency of performers and the organization.

# INTIMIDATION AND EFFICIENCY

**At the start of my career, I got to work for a legend. He was technology's golden boy, an innovation whiz.**

I was excited about the opportunity, feeling it would be a fantastic career move. It wasn't until I moved across the country that I realized I had signed up to work for the devil himself and a textbook example of a jerk.

His office was in my direct line of vision, and I saw people going in and out all day. A pattern quickly emerged: employees entered looking fine but left looking like boxers who had just lost by a knockout. I found the study of this human behavior oddly captivating- until it was my turn to go in.

He said, "Be seated." I relaxed, letting down my guard. "How goes it?" he asked. He seemed genuinely interested. "It's alright," I said. He slammed his fist on the desk and exclaimed, "No, it isn't!" Then he made a buzzer noise, like on a game show. I felt completely powerless.

Now I understood why those people I had seen coming out of his office resembled the other guy after nine rounds with Tyson.

I didn't know what would happen, but I had a good idea. He didn't fire me, but he set the performance bar on my next project higher than I knew a human could jump.

My only refuge was counting the days until the boss was out of town.

---

Generally, the CEO was away from the office multiple days monthly, and once or twice annually, he would take a week or two of vacation. Work and life were good for us in the office during those brief moments. During his absence, the office churned like a well-oiled machine.

Believing in the work, many of us arrived early and worked extended hours, even at night.

There was a sense of collaboration that rarely existed when the CEO was in town. The departments worked together to achieve a common goal. I enjoyed being part of a talented team. We produced impressive results on unique projects.

I clearly remember the episode where I learned the CEO would be away the next day. That night, I slept like an exhausted meerkat hunkered down in my burrow. My stress evaporated as I remembered the despot, with his unpredictable behavior, would be gone for a week.

When I woke up the next day, fresh snow glistened in the morning sun. The place looked magical, like a dream come true, putting me in a joyful mood. Usually, I loathed driving to work, but this day was different. I cheered, knowing the cause of my suffering was far away on a speaking tour.

Bruce Springsteen played loudly through my car's sound system, and I sang along at the top of my lungs, every word to Born to Run.

**I felt invincible!**

As I pulled into the parking garage, I saw the CEO's black Audi A8.

My reptilian brain kicked into overdrive. I contemplated making a run for the border. (Hadn't Springsteen just told me that I was born to run?)

I left my car and went towards the office, filled with apprehension. This reversal of fortune was like a punch to the gut, a wake-up call. Accustomed to daily toxicity, I was numb. It wasn't until I stepped outside the situation that I realized I needed to change. If I didn't, enduring abuse would jeopardize my health. I concluded I could not thrive within that organization.

If only the CEO had stepped back and realized he had hired the best in the business — talented, creative, and collaborative thinkers excited to see his vision come to fruition. However, he believed fear was the best method to manage and control his employees. So, he ruled with an iron fist and a temper that rattled nerves and terrorized even the most steadfast worker.

We all went about our tasks timidly. We left the office deflated, and anxious. Unfortunately, in this oppressive environment, creativity was discouraged, and great ideas were rejected — because they weren't from the wunderkind himself.

> I hope I do a **MEDIOCRE** job today!
>
> - No one, ever

In my experience, people want to feel a sense of pride where they spend most their adult years, their job. Nobody shows up to work and says, "I hope I do at least a mediocre job today." In my experience, people want to succeed at their jobs. However, navigating a challenging job and a jerk boss can eventually take its toll on even the most well-meaning and enthusiastic employee.

During exit interviews, I often hear, "I love my coworkers and clients. I can't stand working for my boss." When I see these same people years later, I often discover they have thrived at another company.

> **Reality Check**
> Journalist Lisa Belkin cites studies showing that people who work with demeaning and disrespectful people tend to call in sick, make fewer suggestions, put in less effort, and produce lower-quality results.

Have you ever wondered if jerks think we should know all the unwritten rules?

---

**Your Next Encounter**

In the next chapter, I'll explain what I mean by those unwritten rules.

---

# THE UNWRITTEN RULE

Here's a personal story about another type of lesson learned from an intimidating boss.

Things were not going as I had expected. Keeping my enthusiasm and spirits up was hard while working in such a toxic environment. I spent most of my time licking my wounds, trying to figure out how to survive another day. This routine wore me out. I gave so much energy to thinking about survival, thriving wasn't even on my radar.

---

*How do I keep myself out of harm's way? What do I need to do to stay safe in this environment?*

---

My mind went from job performance to survival.

It wasn't long after I joined the company that I discovered this jerk's unwritten rule:

---

Employees were expected to get to work before the CEO and stay until after he left.

---

Sometimes that meant a twelve-hour workday. I didn't find my time at the office productive, and it was exhausting. I was done with my work but had to wait for the CEO's departure. Considering my limited morale, I would not do more. I sat at my desk playing solitaire, trying to give the appearance of working.

I could not leave the office, go home, have dinner at a normal hour, get a decent night's sleep, or use those hours to care for myself.

By now, the repercussions of blindly following the unspoken rule should be clear.

Staying put and not fighting back could have made me a victim.

I could slip into martyrdom and take pride in my suffering.

Either way, the quality of my work inevitably declined, and if we were to succeed, someone else on my team would have to make up for it.

---

**Your Next Encounter**

My next example is for those of you who think business travel is glamorous.

*Think again.*

---

# TRAVELING WITH THE CEO JERK

**Here's another situation that guarantees pain and suffering.**

Since my CEO had harshly criticized me during my last performance review, his request that I join him on a business trip came as a surprise. He was going to present the project I'd spent weeks on. I viewed the invitation as an opportunity. I had worked on the project from inception, and now I would watch the CEO present it. My pride of accomplishment would swell when we closed the business with a billion-dollar client.

I got to the airport with time to spare and checked my luggage, a simple pleasure when traveling not having to drag a suitcase through the airport. As I waited at the gate for the CEO, it wasn't long before I spotted him. He looked at me with a murderous glare and said, "Where are your bags?"

His question caught me off guard. "My bags? I checked my bags," I replied.

> *"We don't check bags at this organization. That's what an amateur does."*

Completely stunned, I felt alone in the packed terminal as he continued to berate me for five minutes about my stupidity regarding checking my luggage. He spoke to me like I was a third grader. "We don't check bags. Do you understand?" he insisted.

"Now say it again," he continued with condescension, "Why aren't we checking luggage, Jennifer?"

With an eye roll and a disgusted turn, he boarded the plane.

He didn't explain his anti-bag sentiment, but I assumed it involved making him wait unnecessarily at our destination while I retrieved my bags.

He flew first class, but thankfully I was safely distant in coach.

---

> I thought to myself, "I'm so thankful air travel has a class system!"

---

I couldn't fathom a long flight sitting beside him as he harped about my bags. I was busy getting lost in a book when the captain announced on the intercom that it was safe to move about the cabin. Before I saw my CEO standing over me, I heard his distinctly triggering voice say, "You're on company time, and you will work." When I looked up, he added, "I'll be back to check on you."

He kept his promise and checked on me three more times during the four-hour flight.

He asked for the thirty-page bound report I'd prepared for the meeting. The request surprised me because he had already reviewed and approved the report. He hovered over me, looking at the paper, then told me he wanted to make some changes. He sputtered as I tried to take notes, but I didn't have time to grab a pen or ask him for one. Hopefully, I'd remember.

I opened my laptop and made the changes. That was the simple part.

What's challenging is figuring out how to get twenty-five copies of a thirty-page document printed by 7:00 a.m.

> **Reality Check**
>
> Great leaders not only delegate but also inspire.

By the time we landed, it was almost 9:00 p.m. The CEO followed me to the baggage claim, lecturing me again for being an amateur and checking my bags. Maybe you already guessed that my bags didn't make it. That only fueled his anger. "That is why we do not check bags!" He had a driver waiting for him. "Deal with all this! Get those reports printed and bound. I'll meet you in the hotel lobby tomorrow at 6:00 a.m." With that, he left me at the airport.

My bags did not arrive.

After filing my lost bag report, I went to the hotel, bought the least humiliating clothing I could find in the gift shop, found a local Kinko's, and burned the midnight oil. After grabbing just an hour of sleep the following day, I met the CEO in the lobby. From the look on his face, he wasn't happy.

On the way to the meeting, he didn't say a word. He wouldn't even look at me. I tried to anticipate what might happen next. At the beginning of the client meeting, I distributed the reports, and the CEO announced, "Jennifer will make the presentation and handle all your questions."

I stood before the client and the CEO in my cheap hotel-shop ensemble, my heart pumping from confusion, excitement, and dread.

I took a deep breath and gave the presentation of my career. When it was over, I helped close a multimillion-dollar deal.

I left the meeting ecstatic, but my boss seemed indifferent. When we got to the airport, he finally said, "Now tell me again, why don't we check bags?"

That trip was one of the most stressful experiences in my career.

> **Reality Check**
> Bullying is a form of workplace violence: In 2004, 24.5% of 516 companies surveyed reported bullying during that year, of which employee aggressors were 39.2%, 24.5% customers, and 14.7% supervisors.
> - National Institute for Occupational Safety and Health (NIOSH)

It's unfortunate that I only learned how bad workplace stress was after it hurt me. Workplace stress has adverse effects on mental and physical health. There's a high price, for going along to get along. Even checking bags makes me flinch to this day.

# WORKING FOR A JERK CAN BE DEADLY

**Being battered by an office jerk can seriously affect your health. Now, there are numbers to prove it.**

Researchers at Tel Aviv University conducted a twenty-year study of workplace stress. They tracked 820 people from varied professions who started healthy in 1988. The study looked at the effects of workload, the freedom given to workers to decide how to meet those demands, and social interactions with colleagues and supervisors.

The research revealed that people working with unpleasant colleagues were 2.4 times more prone to death. In those two decades, fifty-three workers passed away, and most reported less peer support at work.

The correlation was strongest between ages thirty-eight and forty-three, and that is completely logical. If you're not running the world, or at least your cubicle pod, by age forty, then it's natural to wonder why.

What's the price of tolerating the jerks in your life?

A toxic work environment degrades productivity, drives away talent, increases turnover and absenteeism, inhibits creativity and problem-solving, and destroys team cohesion.

> **Reality Check**
> A Gallup poll found that only one in five employees agreed that they were strongly motivated to do outstanding work by their management.

Jerks are typically selfish, arrogant, and manipulative people. Their dedication to goals leads to neglecting employee welfare. They trust no one and collaborate only on the surface level. Their bosses are skillfully charmed, oblivious to what's happening, while they disregard the consequences for peers and direct reports.

The result: good people get fed up and leave companies, while jerks get promoted.

> **Reality Check**
> Richard S. Wellins, a senior vice president at Development Dimensions International, who has for thirty-four years provided "anti-bullying training" to business executives, estimates that one in ten bosses tend to bully their employees.

Successful jerks leverage what they have to the fullest. When tall, they might use height to intimidate you. If they're attractive, they may lean on their charisma over skills. If nepotism protects their behavior, they will tell family about your faults.

## JERK BOSSES COST MORE THAN HURT FEELINGS

**People desire to belong to something larger than themselves. Our genetic code implies that tribal belonging is essential.**

So, what happens when we don't feel like our talents are contributing to something bigger?

You have most likely become discouraged when you get worn down — emotionally and physically — daily, showing up to offer your talents only to be deflated by a workplace jerk.

At my biotech client, the manager of the underperforming team treated the team harshly. His preferred leadership style was a mix of Machiavellian fear and a hint of the Tasmanian Devil. The good news is that he was terminated within six months of the first complaint. Unfortunately, high levels of toxicity had already seeped into the culture.

I recently viewed a program concerning Chornobyl wolves on Animal Planet. The topic of the program was how toxic radiation affected a naturally balanced landscape. The parallels to the workplace became apparent to me. A not-so-fun fact is that it can take centuries for the environment to recover from radiation. Eliminating toxic behavior in the workplace may seem like an endless task.

I studied group recovery duration after a toxic disturbance. The rehabilitation of the environment depends on factors such as acknowledging the root cause, removing the sources of trouble, establishing accountability, and committing to a new way.

Humans share similarities with Chornobyl's wolves. They adapt as much as possible within their pack to adjust to challenging environments. But with quadrupeds and bipeds alike, the more we succumb to crippling situations, the more we learn to walk with a limp.

Most people will exert as much energy as possible to cope with their jobs. They may get used to dealing with jerks until their limp becomes immobile. At that point, self-preservation will probably require even the most dedicated team members to leave their positions.

Let's explore my theory and do a quick equation. In the table, rank your responses to the Assessment Questions, and then I'll tell you how you scored.

**How much effort is your workplace losing?**

| Assessment Questions | Your Ranking from 1-5 (1 = low / 5 = high) |
| --- | --- |
| How much of your effort would you give to a supportive and caring boss? | 5 |
| How much of your effort would you give to a caustic, undermining boss? | 1 |
| Subtract the second line from the first and multiply by 10%: 4 x 10 = | 40% |

This formula suggests a toxic manager causes the organization to lose 40 percent of your productivity. One person's actions matter, in this situation, negatively.

# DAVE THE MINDFUL JERK

**The word *mindful* is usually thought of in a positive light, as in mindful meditation or mindfulness.**

The Mindful Jerk gives their full mind to being a jerk.

They know precisely what they are doing. For example, a coworker talks too loudly on the phone. They invade personal space, gossip behind coworkers' backs, tell offensive jokes, and show complete disregard for the sign on the sandwich in the fridge that reads:

---

**I belong to Fran and Fran only. DO NOT EAT ME!**

---

When Fran goes to the lunchroom, she finds her sandwich is gone.

That was Dave—our Mindful Jerk. He put his full mind into being a jerk to everyone. I was in my late twenties working for a small business that had just crossed the tipping point from start-up to "respectable" company.

Dave was not my boss; he was a coworker sitting in the next cubicle. Although someone warned me about his antics, I believe in letting everyone make their own impression. In my first eight hours with Dave, I learned I would need to request a cubicle change immediately. The dreaded ringing of his phone alerted me, as I knew I would soon be annoyed. Pavlov would not have needed more than a day to document my operant response to Dave's voice. He took the call at what must have been one hundred decibels (workplaces average seventy). His conversations were so loud the entire office knew everything, from what he did on the weekends to when his irritable bowels were flaring up again. I could've overlooked this behavior, if it were the only thing he did. But no, he had refined other jerk skills. He told offensive jokes, he spread the "lay-off" rumor, he walked into your cubicle unannounced and staying even after you'd left. If I got a dollar each time I heard, "You going to eat that?" while he gestured at my leftovers, I wouldn't need to bring my lunch; I could buy it every day.

It was a shock when our manager tasked Dave with training Andrew, a new hire. Andrew was twenty-two, fresh out of college, bright-eyed, and eager. This was his first full-time job.

Sensing his youthful innocence, Dave gave Andrew the wrong instructions, from documenting tech updates to working the copier. Once, Dave convinced Andrew that our client Tech Zone was pronounced Tech-Zoney, giving it a South-of-the-Border flair. When Andrew was asked which account he was assigned to, he proudly stated, "Tech Zoney," igniting deep belly laughter from Dave and uncomfortable silence from the customer service team.

The last I heard, Dave became a director at the company. Despite being a jerk, his work was productive. Perhaps because it was a small outfit, management feared they could not afford to lose the business. But they weren't asking *at what cost?*

I've stated that a jerk boss and abusive management can adversely affect productivity and cause high employee turnover. However, in Dave's case, he only became a boss later. We can trace his negative effect on me and other staff members back to his time as a regular team member.

One toxic person can infect an entire team. Also, if team members see jerks get promoted, they may conclude that's what it takes to get ahead.

So, jerks not only discourage staff from speaking up; they can encourage staff to behave like jerks, too.

Quantifying all costs is not as easy as quantifying sales volume or even staff turnover. Some actions have a less apparent outcome, such as fostering a culture of gloom and creating the next generation of jerks.

> **Reality Check**
> "The rotten apple spoils his companions."
>     - Benjamin Franklin

### Your Next Encounter

Have you ever heard a manager say, "Early is on time. On time is late!"?

That rule doesn't apply to some jerks.

# THE TARDY AND UNPREPARED JERK

**The tax season was at its peak for a major Los Angeles tax firm.**

The large office space contained rows of gray desks and filing cabinets instead of walls. Maria prepared for her following client meeting, but he was late again. She was not looking forward to meeting with him. He was typically late and rarely prepared. She was only hoping that he'd finally bring the required documents, allowing her to finalize his file.

Thinking about his last time in the office, she rolled her eyes. He reprimanded her openly as the signing documents were not prepared. Because he didn't give her the data, she couldn't fill out the form early. He seemed blind to his own carelessness as he hurled insults, accusations, and threats.

How long should you wait?

Still holding out hope he might not arrive, Maria glanced at the time on the clock above the door. He was thirty minutes late, and she had another client in the waiting area. She waved her next client over. Almost on cue, as her punctual client walked toward her, the nightmare client came sweeping in with his six-year-old son in tow. As far as she was concerned, he was late and had forfeited his remaining time.

Standing up as he approached, she calmly smiled and requested he make a new appointment. Her request threw the man into a rage. He started demanding his meeting, his voice growing louder with each repeated request. Maria called her manager over to resolve the situation. All the while, the tardy jerk was spewing threats and insults at both the agency and Maria.

The manager asked the man courteously what it would take to de-escalate the situation. In a loud, stern voice, the man insisted, "To have my damn taxes done. Now!"

Maria simply agreed, requested the other client to wait, and directed the angry man to sit.

He smiled proudly, the tardy jerk turned to the boy, "See, son, that is how you get what you want in life."

---

**Your Next Encounter**

Here's another unwritten rule:

*Jerks get to cut the line.*

# THE ENTITLED JERK

**I was at the airport waiting in line to check in for a flight.**

It was the holidays, and the waiting times were longer than normal. It seemed everyone in Los Angeles had booked a flight to New York.

An anxious man was worried he would not make his flight. He stood at the back of the line, groaning. Eventually, he cut in front of the line. With that, the airline employee working at the counter informs him, "Excuse me, sir. You need to go back to the end of the line."

This was like dumping gasoline on a fire. The man was fuming. He shouted:

*"Do you have any idea who I am?"*

The airline agent was calm, got on the speaker, and asked:

> **"Excuse me, does anyone recognize this man? He seems to have forgotten who he is."**

The airline employee handled that jerk with such finesse. His behavior was unjustifiable. Though inexcusable, this person may have adopted the view that important individuals can treat those below them harshly.

I'm still surprised by entitled behavior, at the airport or elsewhere. I couldn't believe my eyes when I saw a woman changing her baby's dirty diaper on a table in the back of a store!

> **BOOK4U**
>
> Emily Maria Zitek,
>
> "Feeling Wronged Leads to Entitlement and Selfishness,"
>
> Stanford University Dissertation (Stanford, 2010)

Frankly, I don't know where this feeling of entitlement started. Not all of these people could be aristocrats or ridiculously rich. Yet, they seem to be exempt from the rules of decorum for some unknown reason.

A study published in the journal *Social Psychological and Personality Science* found that, even though rudeness defies social norms, people who witness this behavior will probably perceive it as a sign of power even though they know it's rude. It seems strange that acting rudely can make you seem important.

> **Reality Check**
> The spin on the Golden Rule says:
> "Those who have the gold make the rules."

Regrettably, many who believe money equals privilege feel this way. Intimidation is often seen as a means to victory by some. Choosing kindness is hard for those who believe winning is everything.

**Your Next Encounter**

The customer is always right. *Always? You serious?*

# THE JERK CUSTOMER

**I'm okay with a demanding customer; it's the unreasonable customer I have a problem with.**

As I shared earlier, we train people in how to treat us. In hindsight, I trained my unreasonable customer to be a jerk.

They called me at all hours, expecting deep discounts and an immediate turnaround of updated proposals.

I jumped through hoops, yet they didn't return my calls within "eight business hours," as promised in their voicemail greetings.

> **Reality Check**
>
> You train people how to treat you.

The Jerk Customer doesn't value your time, what you offer them, or even your point of view.

### Qualities of Jerk Customers

- Keep trying to grind you down on the cost
- Avoid returning calls, then complain of lacking required information
- Doesn't introduce you to other members of their organization
- Complain about poor customer service to your boss — when you don't deserve it — as a way of getting special treatment

It may sound simple, but building relationships of mutual respect from the outset is key — respect proceeds from the value they give to your product or service.

This is a common occurrence with average salespeople. They often lack confidence in going for the close.

They don't seem to convince the customer that *they* have value — and deserve respect.

I have been both the top and the bottom performer on sales teams. At times, I've been highly successful. At others, I was a total failure in my cold-calling efforts. The big difference between the two behaviors is my internal monologue. My mentor challenged me with the following:

*"What is the story I'm telling myself?"*

What we tell ourselves about ourselves decides our behavior. That voice inside our heads must insist that what we're selling has value — and so do we, as capable professionals, who understand customers' needs.

The customer can tell whether we value our products or ourselves. I have witnessed salespeople constantly imploring their managers to offer yet another discount, and I've worked with sales teams that close deals for high prices and continue to win more business. A salesperson who values themselves conveys value, which the customer perceives.

**Heads Up!**

**BE BORING AND THE BEASTS WILL FIND INTEREST ELSEWHERE**

**Why might we think we don't offer or have value for ourselves?**

We may have the mindset that we're at the mercy of customers:

*"If they don't sign the contract, I don't get paid. If I can't pay my mortgage, I will lose everything."*

In brief, we've gone from trying to make a sale to meeting a basic need: shelter. The most challenging mindset of some salespeople I've worked with was their fear that customers would be unreasonable.

By assuming customers are unreasonable, these salespeople are training their prospects to behave like bullies. They're creating jerk customers with their own self-fulfilling prophecy.

> **Reality Check**
> Albert Einstein insisted that, for humans to change our world, which we have created by thinking, we will need to change our thinking.

Self-preservation demands that you value yourself first, appreciate what you're selling, and, by treating your customers with respect, train them to respect you and what you can do for them. Now, consider an example my colleague shared with me. He worked in sales for a demanding boss, but this woman was not a jerk. No, if anything, he sometimes had to convince her not to offer a discount. Her mantra was:

> *"We spoil our customers!* **They'll be afraid to go anywhere else."**

Imagine if respect and value was a two-way street in the sales process. It can be!

# KISS-UP, KICK-DOWN JERKS

According to the 2024 report, "Workplace Bullying Statistics Research & Facts," in the United States, four out of ten employees suffer from some form of workplace bullying, which may come from managers, coworkers, or customers.

Maybe you know these offenders. Their actions rarely match their words. My friend Libby puts it:

---

**"They are incongruent."**

---

These are the colleagues or managers who plaster teamwork slogans on the walls and line their bookshelves with titles from management gurus. They schedule team building off-sites months in advance- yet they're the ones who cancel at the last minute or don't show up at all.

A participant in a program shared:

> My previous manager deliberately created a barrier between me and his boss, covertly presenting my ideas as his. This manipulation was not just about control. The act undermined the team's trust and cohesion, a serious concern for any organization.

This anecdote helped me understand the term *kiss-up, kick-down jerk*.

I have had several opportunities to observe organizations with "kiss-up, kick-down" team members. In one instance, I collaborated with a team where a management position became available. The employee who kissed up and kicked down was selected for the position.

I couldn't understand why at first, since I found this person's behavior obnoxious.

After consulting with the team individually, the consensus was clear: everyone agreed that the person lacked technical skills but excelled at charming leaders. Management mistook that charm for qualification.

---

**How were they deceived?**

---

By exploiting the people under him, the striving jerk presented others' ideas as if they were his own. He fooled upper management, positioning himself for promotion.

Back to the safari theme, this behavior is a top-tier strategy in the animal kingdom. Like the lion, kiss-up, kick-down jerks act like they are at the top of the food chain. They say that all their coworkers are weak. They are assertive to give the impression that they are strong. A slow gazelle is fast food for a hungry lion.

Lions and other big cats, while strong and ferocious, typically pursue the easiest kill. When hunting, they attack the most vulnerable in a herd.

**In short, apex predators are experts at analyzing their prey.**

The team worried this human predator would get a promotion. Concerns arose that the new manager's negative comments would affect their reviews. Project delays also arose from the team's worry regarding their new leader's lack of experience managing tasks.

Most of the team got their resumes ready, while the rest began scheduling interviews. For ten years, this team had been working to develop an effective system. They had proven they could work as a disciplined force comparable to a strategic pack of wolves or a pride of lions. The collapse of that team could be devastating to the company.

When a kiss-up, kick-down person gets promoted, the unfairness of that move may well cause an entire team to leave the organization.

> **Reality Check**
>
> Our world moves so fast that we may assume **NEW** means **BETTER**
>
> But remember: **INNOVATION = RISK!**
>
> If it's truly an innovation, by definition, it hasn't been tried before.

Bruce Tuckman, a management consultant, created the Tuckman Model, which describes group development phases. Only through close collaboration, dedicated effort, and learning from errors can a team become high-performing and earn rewards. It could be years before they perform like experienced groups do now.

The kiss-up and kick-down jerk strategically chooses their peer alliances while dividing their one-on-one transactions along party lines of "above me" and "below me." If you have a corner office, it shows favor. They could ignore or disparage you if you're in the next cubicle. Their body language will communicate either respect or a warning, based on their perception of you.

Here are unmistakable signs of the kiss-up, kick-down behavior:

- Conceals or blames mistakes on subordinates or situations beyond their control
- Keeps their targets under constant stress
- Cultivates power through fear rather than respect
- Withholds information from underlings, keeping the information flow top-down and preventing feedback to upper management
- Blames conflicts and problems on a coworker
- Creates an uncomfortable work environment where people walk cautiously and behave in ways they usually would not

The *Bulletin of the Atomic Scientists* describes Robert McNamara, an American business executive and the eighth United States secretary of defense, as a classic case of the kiss-up, kick-down personality.

- He told senior leadership what they wanted to hear rather than what they should know.
- He was careful not to offend influencers.
- He expected his subordinates to behave toward him the way he kissed up to his bosses.

Jerks are prevalent in business, and they get promoted. The main reason is that some people believe these things are good for profits. They get results. However, as I've pointed out, collateral damage in terms of decreased staff morale and turnover will erode results for the team — and the entire organi-

> **BOOK4U**
>
> John J. Mearsheimer and D. Shapley,
>
> "McNamara's War,"
>
> Bulletin of the Atomic Scientists (Vol. 49, No. 6, 1993)

zation — over the long term.

Also, not only do jerks spawn other jerks who imitate them, but their abusive behavior can turn competent, well-adjusted employees into martyrs or victims.

And it's a vicious cycle: Staff members who resign themselves to being martyrs or victims are apt to encourage jerks. That's because people who don't push back when it's appropriate are easily manipulated.

Having scouted, observed, and documented workplace beasts and behaviors, know that you're not helpless.

As for the wolves of Chornobyl, mutant wolves developed a superpower that could help save human lives. Researchers discovered that the animals living in the Chornobyl Exclusion Zone (CEZ) had been genetically modified to exhibit resistance to cancer.

Is it possible that some of us can transmute our experiences into exhibiting resistance to jerks?

---

**Your Next Encounter**

The next part of this book focuses on how, as responsible professionals, we can work daily to create healthier and more productive environments.

### Three Steps to Jerk Management

When you identify the jerk in yourself:

**1. Pause and Reflect**

Understanding the "why" behind your behavior helps you respond more thoughtfully next time.

Ask yourself:

- What triggered my behavior?
- Was I stressed, overwhelmed, or feeling disrespected?
- Did I misinterpret someone's actions or intentions?

**2. Own It and Apologize**

A sincere, timely apology can go a long way:

"I realize I came off harsh earlier. That wasn't fair to you, and I'm sorry."

Avoid justifying or blaming — just acknowledge and move forward.

**3. Identify Patterns**

Keeping a journal or mental log can help you spot and manage these patterns.

- Do certain people or situations trigger you?
- Are you more reactive when you're tired or hungry?

**When you identify the Jerk in those around you:**

**1. Recognize the Behavior**
Understanding that their behavior is about them, not you, helps you stay grounded.

**2. Don't Take the Bait**
Stay calm and composed. Jerks often feed off emotional reactions. Use neutral, professional language — even if they don't.
Example: "Let's keep this focused on the issue, not personal attacks."

**3. Set Boundaries**
You can be direct and respectful. Let them know what behavior is unacceptable.
Example: "I'm happy to discuss this, but not if it's going to be disrespectful."

# IDENTIFY THE HYBRID

Refer to the chart below if you can't neatly put someone in one of the three boxes of MVJ. Pay close enough attention, and you will see which traits are dominant and which are secondary.

*For example:*
- A jerk who doesn't want to be labeled a bully can promote themselves as a martyr to justify their prosecution; this is the Jartyr.

- A Verk is a victim who becomes a jerk out of resentment. Their primary driver is victimhood, and reactive nature is one of a jerk.

| The Punnett Square* | | MARTYR (m) | VICTIM (v) | JERK (j) |
|---|---|---|---|---|
| | MARTYR (M) | Mm=Martyr | Mv=Mictim | Mj=Merk |
| | VICTIM (V) | Vm=Vartyr | Vv=Victim | Vj=Verk |
| | JERK (J) | Jm=Jartyr | Jv=Jictim | Jj=Jerk |

*A diagram used to predict the genotypes of a particular cross or breeding experiment will help identify the hybrid subject matters.

| Identified ☐ | Check this box when you feel confident that you have identified a hybrid, including yourself. |
|---|---|

Now we have the skills to identify each of the MVJ types. They are not genetic mutations but choices anyone might make each day. Let's see how their behaviors can be tamed.

Let's learn to get along!

PART FIVE

## WHERE DO WE GO FROM HERE?

*Two roads diverged in a wood, and I —
I took the one less traveled by,
And that has made all the difference.*

- Robert Frost

## GET YOUR BEARINGS

**We should check your readiness and path before you bravely venture into the wild.**

Let's visit our territorial map. Can you spot at least three traits from each of our archetypes in their respective territories?

We start by inspecting our equipment and ourselves. We must understand our strengths and weaknesses prior to engaging with bullies, stragglers, and the wounded.

Suppose at any point the things and conditions that surround you may be so threatening that your own mental or physical health could be at risk. Then, maybe you should think about drastically changing course, for you and maybe the whole team.

> **Reality Check**
> Please understand: This book is no substitute for professional help. Your company's HR department or mental-health professionals should be consulted if problems seem insurmountable. We all need caregiving and support from time to time. Don't hesitate to ask for help if you feel the problem is serious and you can't deal with it on your own.

It's easier to decide to change than to actually change. Now, after days of trekking, I won't be asking you to eat spoiled rations and risk food poisoning. But I will ask you to smell your sandwiches before we set out- so you know what spoiled food smells like and can recognize it again.

Maybe you saw traits of martyrs, victims, and jerks reflected in yourself at different times. It's also crucial to recognize it as a dynamic process.

> **Heads Up!**
>
> **SHOOTING WITH ANYTHING BUT A CAMERA WILL LAND YOU IN JUNGLE JAIL!**

Interactions and transactions can involve shifting roles. Jerks exploit those who are martyrs and victims. Also, by persisting in their roles, those abused creatures will offer themselves as nourishment for a growing population of jerk predators.

So, in the next chapter, let's begin with individual assessment.

# CONDUCTING YOUR OWN SELF-ASSESSMENT

**It is time for a radical gut check!**

### Radical Gut Check

I want to make sure you're ready for this. After all, tour guides rarely get great reviews if a member of the group doesn't make it back to camp. Before you can change yourself or your circumstances, I suggest a radical gut check (RGC) process.

The RGC is a self-assessment to identify your current behavioral tendencies. You might not be showing up as a martyr, a victim, or a jerk all the time or even most days. You might not have yet fallen into those behaviors as a habit.

However, it will be helpful for you to see negative behaviors in yourself before you turn your attention to your teammates, your supervisor, or your workplace in general.

By now, you probably think you can spot MVJ traits in those around you. And you may be thinking, *Oh, not me, ever!* But I encourage you to take your binoculars, turn them around, and look back at yourself.

**How Do You React to Bullies?**

One of the most likely reasons people turn to this book is for advice on dealing with a jerk, usually a boss. How you've coped with that behavior says a lot about your attitude. Write down the numbers of these statements that resonate with you.

Have you ever said to yourself:

1. I go along to get along, and then it all catches up with me.
2. I am uncomfortable with conflict and usually avoid it.
3. I won't take the blame for a teammate's poor performance. They are either not up to the job, or they misunderstood my instructions.
4. I have tried to speak up, but my anxiety has turned me into a kid who was always insecure and bullied.
5. Being pushy is the only way to get ahead.
6. I feel I'm being abused, but I don't see any way out of the situation.
7. I feel stuck in my job. I don't see pathways to promotion.
8. I admire people who can forcefully "persuade" others.
9. I deserve credit for the team's achievements if I'm the team leader.

10. The deck is stacked against me. If I give it extra effort, I'll just get knocked down.
11. Results are all that matter. My advice to complainers is to suck it up and get on with the job.
12. I don't set boundaries. I don't push back if the boss asks for more than I can give. Someday, they will notice how much I am giving.

The following table shows the connection between MVJ behaviors and the numbered statements. Don't be surprised if, at one time or another, you've entertained each of these behaviors. Almost certainly, you've seen coworkers behave as if they thought that way — though they might not be self-aware enough to make a change.

Again, the trap is whether these behaviors become your habitual response to troublesome situations.

| Habitual Behavior Type | Typical Responses to Questions |
| --- | --- |
| **MARTYR** | 2, 4, 12 (and any of the Victim responses) |
| **VICTIM** | 1, 4, 6, 7, 8, 10 |
| **JERK** | 3, 5, 8, 9, 11 |

Carl Jung says our biggest issues with others are usually our unresolved problems, fears, and insecurities projected onto them. We become angry when we secretly fear any accusation or criticism that is true about ourselves.

Recognizing these qualities is the first step to discarding them. Insight also gives us a glimpse into why they appear in those around us.

If more of your responses fall into the jerk category, the next section is especially for you. (But I'd advise the rest of you not to skip it!)

### The Beast That Lurks Within

Our nervous system relies on a reptilian brain. This primitive system is present in all mammals. The reptilian brain underlies our logical thinking, yet the snake's drives can overpower the wisdom of our conscious mind.

Based on your responses in the previous section, it will be no surprise that a jerk lurks inside most of us.

- Perhaps our Inner Jerk is released in an episode of road rage or through an unsavory response in the comment section of a blog post.
- Perhaps your Inner Jerk is released or suppressed when an idea you have been spearheading is shot down during the "safe" team brainstorming session, turning spit balling into a game of corporate dodgeball.

Even the calmest people I've met have a boiling point. My tour guide in South Africa seemed kindhearted most of the time, but don't interrupt her when she is speaking about the impressive speed of a cheetah.

The good news is that we can cage, tame, and even release the lurking jerks. Their ferocity can be channeled into creative energy. With consistent, healthy habits, the beast's trainer- that's you- can transform a toxic habitat into a healthier one.

> **BOOK4U**
>
> *John Simons,*
>
> *"Companies Wake Up to the Problem of Bullies at Work; Nearly Two-Thirds of Americans Reported Being Bullied at Work Last Year,"*
>
> *Wall Street Journal (November 15, 2017)*

# ASKING YOURSELF THE KEY QUESTIONS

**Enough with the throat clearing and the pep talk. It's time to ask yourself the tough questions.**

Previously, you evaluated statements to see if you lean M, V, or J. Now, let's survey which situations trigger those behaviors in you.

**Self-Control Is Self-Preservation**

To survive amid intense conflict, one must control reactions.

This function allows a rational response rather than a quick, emotional one.

> **Reality Check**
>
> What is the performance metric for a
>
> **NICE PERSON?**

**There are two aspects of self-awareness:**

- On one hand, you are encountering and identifying MVJs.
- On the other hand, you behave like an M, a V, a J — or some combination of the three. (Refer again to the Punnett Square.)

Quite simply, if you can see what you're doing, you can choose to act differently — and more constructively. And once you learn to do that for yourself, you can develop tactics for encouraging and motivating others to change their behaviors.

### Individual Assessment Checklist

Responding to the following questions will suggest the situations that trigger the MVJ in you. Ask yourself:

### When Do I Act Like a Martyr?

- Have you ever refused to accept responsibility for the decisions that have caused others to suffer?
- Do you actively campaign that you are righteous and self-sacrificing?
- Do you regularly feel you are the only one willing to sacrifice for the cause?
- Do you have a tough time saying "no" and setting personal boundaries?
- Are you exhausted from picking up the pieces for everyone else?

- Do you feel you "die a thousand deaths" more than once a week?
- Are you reluctant to take the initiative to solve your problems?
- Do you seek — even thrive on — appreciation, recognition, and attention?

### When Do I Act Like a Victim?

- Are you quick to blame other people and situations for what does not work in their lives?
- How many minutes/hours of complaining do you do each week?
- Do you become angry at the people or events whom you think have "done you wrong"?
- Does it feel like the world is against you at least once a week?
- Do you often feel justified or self-righteous?
- Do you feel others are mainly responsible for your suffering?
- Do you lack resilience, even from minor setbacks?
- Do those small reversals make you furious? How many "poor me" moments do you experience each week?

### When Do I Act Like a Jerk?

- Do you often feel as though intimidating or coercing others is the only way to get things done?
- Do people look nervous when you enter the room? In

meetings, do you interrupt speakers before they've made their point?
- Do you raise your voice or make your body language "bigger" to make your point?
- Do you talk loudly on the phone even when coworkers can hear you?
- If a coworker is behind a closed door or on the phone, must you assert yourself to get their attention when you think the matter is urgent?
- How much do coworkers' opinions about you affect your decisions?
- Does it matter if they don't respect you as long as they get it done?

**Your Self-Assessment for Self-Awareness**

If you engage in any of these behaviors more than half the time, pay close attention to the actions that lead up to the behavior. If you realize you have been in denial, the rest of us (who are already there) welcome you to join our quest for a more humane environment.

| **Heads Up!**<br><br>ALWAYS<br>MAINTAIN<br>A<br>SAFE<br>PERIMETER | Thoughtful self-assessment is the first step to improving your relationships, performance, and well-being in the workplace. Managing your responses to adversity — being able to apply thoughtful solutions instead of blind reactions — is a sign of *emotional intelligence*. |
|---|---|

This model, introduced by Daniel Goleman, focuses on emotional intelligence as a set of skills that drive human connection. Goleman's model outlines four key elements:

- **Self-awareness** is the ability to read one's emotions and recognize their impact while using gut feelings to guide decisions. Your self-assessment should increase your self-awareness.
- **Self-management** involves controlling one's emotions and impulses and adapting to changing circumstances.
- **Social awareness** is the ability to sense, understand, and react to others' emotions while comprehending social networks.
- **Relationship management** is the ability to inspire, influence, and develop others while managing conflict.

### Your Self-Awareness Has Expanded

If you've already challenged yourself with the foregoing questions, you've worked through the self-awareness step.

### You know the stuff — now apply it!

### Practicing Self-Management

Self-management can begin after self-awareness. When you notice unproductive behaviors in yourself — along with undesired consequences — ask yourself:

> **"Did I bring it with me, or did it bring it out of me?"**

You may have heard the saying: "No matter where you go, you take yourself with you." We may believe and even have proven how strong we are, yet some conditions cause the fiercest of us to take on the role of martyr or victim.

Or maybe you switch to jerk mode in retaliation, on the assumption the best defense is a preemptive offense.

Remember, I cautioned you about the consequences of eating those spoiled rations in your lunchbox. Imagine your current workplace habitat like a buffet. Some selections include your favorite foods (projects or people you gain energy from interacting with). Other dishes might look appetizing but have become toxic (Commiserating Martyrs, Complaining Victims, or Harassing Jerks). And no matter who or what you decide to take in, some options will come with regret as an aftertaste!

What are you putting on your plate? Will we have to call for air support? (Fun fact: Emergency rescues usually start at $10,000 — unless you or your tour guide has taken out special insurance to cover it!)

Of course, it's not just about avoiding food that might make you sick. Protecting your well-being and maintaining good mental health also means sidestepping minor annoyances- and not letting them get to you.

## Developing Social Awareness

You've thought about your actions and how you typically respond when triggered. Now, for the next step, it is time to expand your attention to your surroundings. Social awareness starts when you notice how your behavior affects people.

As an aid to surveying your surroundings, practice what the military calls *situational awareness*. A reconnaissance force surveying a dense jungle can't expect foes to line up in front of them. They must also remain on the lookout for bystanders, who might or might not be noncombatants. Especially with today's advanced technologies, a field force can use sensors that give them eyes on the backs of their heads. Drones circling above the engagement give them the big picture from above, and they can zoom in on areas of interest.

These capabilities give every patrol member heightened awareness of the situation from moment to moment. From their 360-degree viewpoint, they can see potential threats before they are confronted.

Copying the traits of the animal kingdom, rather than reacting to trouble after it appears, they may rely on their defensive tactics training to avoid the danger altogether.

Active situational awareness can prevent conflict in combat and in the office by providing advance information about risks before engagement occurs.

But remember, your response to a threat doesn't always mean avoidance. Sometimes, harm comes directly at you.

*When you deal with conflict constructively, you will expand your skill set.*

Consider the wry wisdom of civil rights activists in the 1960s who knew they were under surveillance by law enforcement:

> **Paranoia is just a heightened state of awareness.**

Which means:

> **Developing situational awareness is essential to self-preservation in the workplace.**

Stay alert to the situation and its context. Taking responsibility for your surroundings starts with taking inventory of your current state and how you got there.

**The next time you find yourself in a troublesome situation at work, ask yourself:**

- How did I arrive at this job? On this team? On this task?
- How aligned am I with the organization's mission?
- Do I think it has a chance of success? Why or why not? What could I do about it?
- How well am I aligned with others in my cohort and collaborations — including leaders, managers, teammates, clients, and other stakeholders? Are we all striving toward the same goal? Are some out only for their own interests?
- How do the leaders in my organization reflect on me? Do I admire them? Do I assume their directives are wise? Effective?
- How do the leaders in my organization reflect on others? Do clients trust them? Is our organization perceived as a problem solver?
- Even if things started off fine, did I fail to recognize some changes that could have been made along the way?
- If we're in a bind now, would we be there if I hadn't kept my mouth shut?

Take time to identify what may not be aligned with your gut sense of professional behavior.

### What ownership do you take when it comes to your situation?

Also, appearances can be deceiving. I've seen impressive, stylish corporate lobbies that turn out to be little more than fronts for dysfunctional and sometimes toxic workplaces. The principles we live by don't shape the surroundings we experience as an organization's culture.

Recently, I noticed my clients' lobby for the first time in years. It caught me off guard as I walked into what I remembered as a dated 1980s-style marble green lobby; instead, I was jolted by the sight of bright yellow, modernist decor. When I asked my clients about it, they commented, "We want Gen Zs to think we are innovative and progressive." I said nothing, but we both know the culture of our ecosystems goes beyond replacing dated marble walls with standing desks and micro-brewed coffee.

> **Heads Up!**
>
> **PROCEED WITH CAUTION**

Some of our habitats are challenging to describe beyond the color of the walls or the style of our office furniture. When I asked a client to explain their company culture, it left them spewing enough buzzwords to fill a tech dictionary.

## Take Ownership of Your Surroundings

Your corporate culture will affect you, and your behavior will affect your team. Over time, the decisions and actions of you and your coworkers will create the corporate climate you are in.

Your thoughts, attitudes, and behaviors are influenced by and influence the culture — all day, every day.

Martyrs and victims might believe they're just bystanders. Jerks may believe they can impose a fear-based culture on everyone else — or at least use others in ways to further their ambitions.

Responsible corporate citizens understand the first rule of responsibility:

> **If you have a complaint, address it first and only to the person who can take action.**

You may disagree with the organization's direction, but if you constantly complain to your open-space neighbor, you are part of the problem.

If you find the company's stated corporate values aren't being lived by, what are you doing to change it? You don't have to be the CEO to affect the surrounding mood. Perhaps the situation is so toxic that you'd be better off finding work elsewhere. If not, it's the old put up or shut up!

Whether you have determined it is time to emigrate or that you want to remain in your current habitat, the next step is all about how you — no matter what position in the organization or your span of authority — can do to make things better for yourself, your team, and your organization.

# CONDUCTING A WORKPLACE ASSESSMENT

**You should now be ready to step back and take in the entire landscape.**

You'll want to better understand the current health — or lack of it — in the prevailing mood, commitment to goals, sense of mission, quality of leadership, and ongoing corporate culture.

In this investigation, you will inevitably identify martyr, victim, and jerk behaviors. Of course, you may already sense them — that's probably why you opened this book.

> **Reality Check**
>
> A Pitch Deck is a slide show used to sell an idea or product by showing rather than telling - and as concisely as possible.

You can't be entirely objective. You are, after all, engaged in the thick of it. You can only watch how you, people, and things around you act. Then, you decide the extent of changes you can and want to make.

As you know, you must begin with yourself.

## Document Your Journey

Your Workplace Assessment can't be done overnight. Yes, you've already encountered problems and endured consequences, but now you will look at situations in the wild with your powerful field glasses.

Allow about ninety days for this activity — longer if you feel the need and can devote the effort. Keep a journal of your interactions with leadership, management, and coworkers.

When you encounter problems, describe them in a scenario. The following table's format should help you capture the information you will need to guide your steps. Complete the form for each potentially troublesome event you observe.

### Workplace Assessment Scenario #[XX, date: time]

**Example** Describe the problematic event in one or two sentences.

**Research** Consult this book and possibly also the References in the end matter to provide background. Characterize the behaviors you observe, especially actions that might be counterproductive, destructive, or even abusive.

**Story** Bear in mind you can never know what's in people's heads or all the contributing factors. Write your own story about how and why this happened. This description will be theoretical, but your interpretation of events and how they affect you are all you have to go on until you decide to seek counsel or help from someone else—someone who, besides yourself, also has the ability to implement changes.

**Life Hack** So, what can you do about it? Write down the possibilities, determine your potential and responsibilities, and state clearly the actions you will undertake.

## TAKING ACTION — YOUR FIELD GUIDE

**Perhaps you've noticed we haven't covered the fourth element of Goleman's model: relationship management.**

Your relationships with the people in your surroundings make up the area where you can create the most.

Your interactions and their outcomes stem from others' perceptions of you. As individuals, based on your behavior toward them and your teammates, they will form their own stories about your personality, your skills, and your emotional intelligence. They will evaluate you based on generosity versus stinginess, clarity versus confusion, capability versus clumsiness, and compassion versus indifference.

> **Reality Check**
> Author Maya Angelou famously shared that, by your actions, you train people how to treat you.

Depending on their situational awareness, they will have an opinion about whether you are intently present or clueless.

You can improve the quality and results of your interactions by shifting your coworkers' beliefs of you. To achieve this, I'll suggest a formal discipline with proven effectiveness: *perception management*.

### Perception Management

Perception management is a term that originated during World War II. The stakes were incredibly high, history is well-known, but you may not know how the Allies developed and implemented a perfect plan of deception.

> **BOOK4U**
>
> Michael Keane,
>
> *Patton: Blood, Guts, and Prayer*,
>
> Regnery History (New York, 2012)

Allied forces had limited resources, so only one invasion into France was possible to fight the German enemy occupying the land. US General George Patton's Third Army used a ruse to make the German command overestimate Allied forces' strength.

In the summer of 1944, prior to moving his tanks into enemy territory, Patton's plan created false perceptions of overwhelming force.

He positioned fifty inflatable tank replicas within a few hundred yards of the front line. To complete the illusion, he surrounded them with trucks outfitted with loudspeakers that broadcast radio chatter and the sounds of tanks and troop movements entering the battle zone. The thunderous clatter carried for fifteen miles.

Patton's perception management plan became known as the "Ghost Army." The enemy was duped, assuming the invaders were in the wrong location. Patton's army took a different route and caught his opponents by surprise, evading their defenses and racing eastward, across France and toward the ultimate victory in Berlin.

Tactics of effective perception management don't require you to pose as someone you're not. I'm not asking you to show up as a decoy. Instead, having a perception management plan can control how others see you. You have the power to reshape their perception of you using self-control and intentional actions. Their actions toward you will likely be different after this.

> **BOOK4U**
>
> Christopher Klein,
>
> "The Top-Secret WWII Unit That Fooled the Nazis,"
>
> WWII Cryptography
>
> Wikipedia
>
> (March 3, 2022)

The result can be to reframe a problem situation — first, to make your team aware of it, then to help guide them in a more positive direction.

### Your Perception Management Plan — A PATH to Success

I'm going to coin a term here to avoid confusion. PM is generally understood to mean program or project management, and PMP is a professional certification in today's workplace.

So, I'm proposing a different term for your perception management plan: PATH — perception awareness technology for health — in the workplace or in any group you're involved in where you want to have more positive and decisive impacts.

You may be surprised that your overall approach to all three MVJ characters can begin with the system I'm calling PATH. I have used this process in organizations throughout the globe, at different levels, and in different industries. Over the years, thousands of individuals have developed, applied, and achieved results from PATH — an approach for deliberately managing how you are being perceived and ultimately managing your well-being.

You may think,

**"I want to know how to deal with them, not what I need to change."**

I must tell you how we show up in the equation. Consider the following processes, their interactions, and the results they generate.

**Perception** How someone sees, hears, senses, and interprets a moment, event, or experience.

**Attitude** Preexisting beliefs filter a perception, instantly forming the observer's attitude toward the event.

**Behavior** What the other person does or says. Their behavior affects your interpretation, your attitude, and then your own behavioral response — and the process continues.

Now consider how this interaction goes back and forth (cause and effect) between two people in an interaction. If you want to change the effect, we need to change the stimuli.

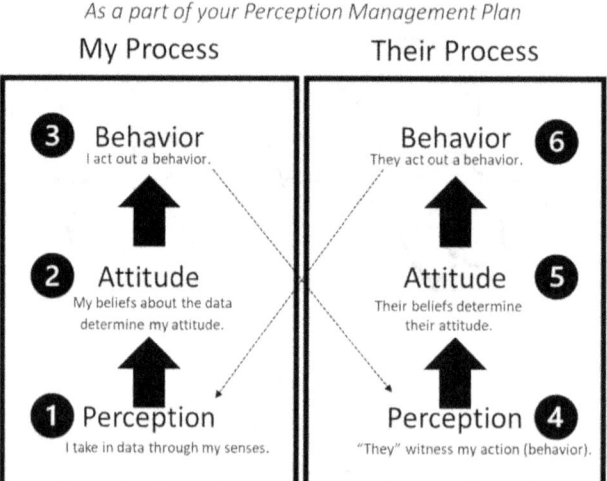

**First: Deliberately manage how you want to be perceived.**

Based on the principle of training others to perceive you, if MVJs are showing up in a way that hasn't worked for you, then you must retrain them on how you want them to interact with you.

- Based on your Self-Assessment, you know how you have been showing up:
    - *What traits do you need to shed?*
    - *How can you embody qualities of cooperation and confidence?*
- Elements of behavioral change can include:
    - Being more assertive — or less defensive — in your body language.
    - Speaking to sound confident in your pace, tone, and volume.
    - Being clear about whom you are addressing in a group discussion.
    - Maintaining eye contact when you're speaking.
- In your mindset, demonstrate well-considered logic and opinions.
    - Express informed opinions based on research:
        - Have you studied the project's requirements?
        - Do you understand the customer's business needs?
- Are you prepared to respond (not react) to jerk behavior to retrain them on how to treat you? For example, if a jerk tries to intimidate you, consider the following responses:
    - *"I don't respond to that tone."*
    - *"This disrespect will not work for me."*

- - The best response I've seen and practiced is just pure silence to their behavior. It is much harder in practice than in words.
- Ask yourself:
  - *Do I always need to be right?*
  - It may surprise you, but needing to be right may also spark a continuous desire to make others wrong, a tactic frequently used by bullies.

**Next: Take ownership of your surroundings.**

Surroundings encompass not only physical space but also the entire *context* of workplace behaviors, embodying corporate mission and culture.

A team is an interactive social network. The iterative processes of perception, attitude, and behavior govern your interactions with your coworkers and your team's behavior.

Taking ownership of your surroundings begins with self-assessment and extends to understanding what changes and affects you can make on others' behaviors.

**Reality Check**

Consider how you want to be perceived.

Speak and act based on how you want to be perceived.

Notice how you get different reactions when you show up differently.

**That's your PATH, your way forward.**

**You can choose to make a difference!**

## TOWARD A HEALTHIER AND HAPPIER WORKPLACE

**With the information in this book, you should be able to guide change in your life and create a better workplace ecosystem — for yourself and others.**

When you realize you can have influence and decide to take action, it is essential to be completely honest.

*It was a brave step undertaking the Individual Self-Assessment.*

You can now see how increased awareness of your surroundings can help you manage conflict, potentially spotting pitfalls. Sometimes, the best choice is to refuse engagement with the beasts- whether they're after your lunch, or you.

Taking corrective actions will require practice, patience, and persistence. Being in control of your emotions and actions is fantastically empowering. Sensing your teammates' emotional states is also bound to improve your interactions.

> **Reality Check**
>
> This old advice still works:
>
> **Praise in public**
>
> **Criticize in private**

---

*It will take time to achieve lasting results.*

---

Recall that the fourth element of the Goleman model is relationship management. At its basis, a workplace is a network of professional and personal relationships. It's a hierarchy of work roles and responsibilities.

Also, if the workplace is failing — if productivity or quality is down, or if only some are thriving — then broaden your perspective beyond your team to understand the larger context. Ask yourself:

What do I need to do for *me* now?

---

As we kick back in the communal tent after the thrills of our daylong safari, help yourself to a libation! You've earned it. Reflect that you had the foresight and the courage to undertake this journey. You were conscientious about closely observing and analyzing the fascinating behaviors of martyrs, victims, and jerks in the wild.

You found the courage to reflect.

Perhaps you were surprised, but you became wiser by recognizing some similar traits in yourself, even if they are not yet habits.

**Whew! Ready to get back to work?**

Consider how far you have come before you and your cohort race for the chargers to retrieve your phones and check for urgent messages.

Think about your next steps on this journey.

You now appreciate that the only human you know who has the power to build a happier workplace and a kinder, gentler planet is the one holding this copy of the book!

---

**Congratulations, <u>you</u> are now being released back into the wild!**

---

# TOWARD A HEALTHIER AND HAPPIER WORKPLACE

# REFERENCES AND FURTHER READING

Aldrich, Nancy M.A., "Taming the Difficult Employee," *Illinois Parks and Recreation* (2002). [http://www.lib.niu.edu/2002/ip020522.html].

Amy, Joyce, "Big Bad Boss Tales; Overbearing Management Styles are all the Rage. Did we Say Rage?" *The Washington Post* (May 29, 2005) *ProQuest*. (Accessed May 28, 2018.)

Belkin, Lisa, "Working for a Boss Who Bullies," *New York Times*, Late Edition - East Coast (May 8, 2005) *ProQuest*. (Accessed May 16, 2018.)

Bradberry, Travis, "How Complaining Rewires Your Brain for Negativity," *TalentSmart*. [http://www.talentsmart.com/articles/How-Complaining-Rewires-Your-Brain-for-Negativity-2147446676-p-1.html].

Cappelli, Giulia, *Find Peace on Purpose: The Intentional Transformation from Blaming to Being* (Independently Published, 2024).

Cianciolo, Jerry, "A Substitute for 'Complaint Free Wednesday,'" *Wall Street Journal,* Eastern Edition (November 21, 2017) *ProQuest.* (Accessed January 1, 2019.)

Dawson, Rachel Shattock, "Office Martyrdom is an Addiction. It's a Black Hole of Disappointment, Resentment, and Anger," *Stylist.* [https://www.stylist.co.uk/life/careers/are-you-the-office-martyr/9172].

Gallup, "Performance Measures That Motivate Employees" (2017). [http://www.gallup.com/workplace/231659/performance-measures-motivate-madden-employees.aspx].

Keane, Michael, *Patton: Blood, Guts, and Prayer,* Regnery History (New York, 2012).

Killoren, Robert, "The Toll of Workplace Bullying," *Research Management Review,* Vol. 20, No. 1, (2014).

Klein, Christopher, "The Top-Secret WWII Unit That Fooled the Nazis," (March 3, 2022.) [https://en.wikipedia.org/wiki/World_War_II_cryptography].

Mearsheimer, John J., and D. Shapley, "McNamara's War," *Bulletin of the Atomic Scientists,* Vol. 49, No. 6, (1993), pp. 18–24. [http://mearsheimer.uchicago.edu/pdfs/A0020x1.pdf].

Mayo Clinic Staff, "Self-Esteem Check: Too Low, Too High, or Just Right?" *Mayo Clinic.* [https://www.mayoclinic.org/healthy-lifestyle/adult-health/in-depth/self-esteem/art-20047976].

Simons, John, "Companies Wake Up to the Problem of Bullies at Work; Nearly Two-Thirds of Americans Reported Being Bullied at Work Last Year," *Wall Street Journal* (November 15, 2017) *ProQuest.* (Accessed May 7, 2018.)

Swartz, Tracy, "Office Bullies," *Chicago Tribune,* (April 21, 2008.) [https://search.proquest.com/docview/420653999].

Workplace Bullying Institute, "2021 Workplace Bullying Statistics Report" (January, 2024.) [https://workplacebullying.org/wp-content/uploads/2024/01/2021-Full-Report.pdf].

Zitek, Emily Maria, "Feeling Wronged Leads to Entitlement and Selfishness," Stanford University Dissertation, (Stanford, 2010.) [http://purl.stanford.edu/yk940fj0071].

# ACKNOWLEDGMENTS

I would like to express my deepest gratitude to my family and friends for their unwavering support and encouragement throughout this journey.

To my mother, your unwavering love, endless support, and boundless wisdom have been the guiding light in my life. This book is a testament to your strength and the inspiration you've given me every day. Thank you for believing in me and for being my greatest teacher. To my father, you have taught me how to be adaptable, independent, and resilient by shaping our home in alignment with the Marine Corps' values. Thank you for your service to our country and our family. To my brother, Tom, you were my best friend growing up. Thank you for being an exceptional big brother and the funniest human I know. With all my love.

Temperance and Kody, the joy you bring into my life lights the way to finish projects such as this book.

I also owe my profoundest thanks to my colleagues who unknowingly served as models for Martyrs, Victims, and Jerks. Jerks, most especially! Whether they supported me, challenged me, or flat out acted like jerks, each helped me grow.

Thank you to my team at AU. You are a brilliant group of peers from whom I learn daily.

Thanks to my editor, Gerald Everett Jones, as well as to La Puerta Productions for cover design and page layouts. Jason Letts did a thorough and thoughtful copyedit. Adero Joan Cate researched reference works and citations. And I'm so impressed with Dr. Christopher Zeineh's illustrations! His work is both expressive and amusing.

A special thank-you to Jo Ann Collins Eck for showing up as a dear friend as I grieved the loss of my beloved Koda during the final stages of this book.

And let me hear from you!

JENNIFER THOMPSON info@nomvj.com

TIME4THOMPSON https://nomvj.com

# ABOUT THE AUTHOR

Jennifer Thompson, Principal, Silverstrand Group and Time4Thompson publishing.

As a founding member of Silverstrand Group, Jennifer Thompson has developed a unique approach to behavior change that includes research and real-world application.

Jennifer applies her background in information processing to the interworking of the human brain to facilitate individuals with upgrading their own unique operating systems.

For over 20 years, Jennifer has been aiding organizations in achieving their strategic goals. With a background that includes sales, management, instructional design, and facilitation, she has had the opportunity to work with a wide range of industries around the globe. This experience has allowed Jennifer to identify the silver strand that weaves through every human interaction, which is perception is reality.

Therefore, by managing the two-way street of perception, we can significantly affect results. After working with leading training and development companies, Jennifer aligned herself with other thought leaders in the industry to form Silverstrand Group.

The simple principle that when we know better, we do better drives Jennifer to continue to expand her understanding of what makes human interaction more effective.

While Jennifer's obsession is the human brain, her passion is being a change agent for humans and animals. She lives in the mountains of Tehachapi, CA where she enjoys flying RC (radio controlled) airplanes, and is the Vice President of her flying club (Tehachapi Crosswinds). Jennifer is a devoted dog mom who has spent the last ten years working with wolves and wolf dogs, educating the public on the magnificence of these beautiful animals.

www.ingramcontent.com/pod-product-compliance
Lightning Source LLC
Chambersburg PA
CBHW070146100426
42743CB00013B/2825